Consider Poor ♡

This heart with a little one in it,
Is to give you to understand,
That hearts can be united.

NANCY LUCE, *1860*

BY WALTER MAGNES TELLER

The Farm Primer
Roots in the Earth (with P. Alston Waring)
Starting Right with Sheep
An Island Summer
The Search for Captain Slocum: A Biography
The Voyages of Joshua Slocum (editor)
Five Sea Captains (editor)
Area Code 215: A Private Line in Bucks County
Cape Cod and the Offshore Islands
Joshua Slocum
Twelve Works of Naive Genius (editor)
Walt Whitman's Camden Conversations (editor)
On the River -- A Variety of Canoe & Small Boat
Voyages (editor)

Consider Poor I

THE LIFE AND WORKS OF NANCY LUCE

WALTER MAGNES TELLER

Reprinted by
The Martha's Vineyard Museum
Edgartown, Massachusetts

We hope that this reprint of Walter Magnes Teller's
Consider Poor I, about the life and work of Nancy Luce,
will satisfy the strong demand for information about
this fascinating woman. Nothing has been changed
from the original 1984 edition.

Since 1984 the Dukes County Historical Society has
become the Martha's Vineyard Museum. Everything
referenced in the book as in the collection of the
Society remains in the collection of the Museum.

ISBN: 978-1-4290-9315-6

For information contact The Martha's Vineyard Museum,
P.O. Box 1310, Edgartown, Massachusetts 02539
www.mvmuseum.org

Contents

It seems to me. . . that nobody should write poetry to exhibit intellect or attainment. Who cares for that sort of poetry? Who cares for learning -- who cares for fine words in poetry? And who does not care for feeling -- real feeling -- however simply, even rudely expressed?

Charlotte Brontë, *Shirley*, Chapter 12

To The Reader

THE subtitle of this book explains its purpose -- to describe a certain woman's life and present her poems -- to dust off and rescue from near oblivion an estimable person and poet.

A denizen of Martha's Vineyard when it first became a summer resort, Nancy Luce was widely known on the Island -- and off-Island, to an extent. Having been thwarted in the usual ways of creation and fulfillment, she had found her outlets in writing, painting, decorating, and in her family of domestic animals. "The hen lady," people called her. Physically sick -- perhaps mentally too -- she was looked on as an eccentric. Very few in those days set much store by her.

But viewing her in the perspective of time, let us give Nancy Luce her due. From early on she was an entrepreneur. Though feminism was not in her vocabulary, she practiced social and economic equality of the sexes. In an age when many could only make their mark instead of signing their names, she wrote a beautiful hand. In an environment where few women lived alone, she did; self-reliant and fearless -- writing, publishing, and selling her booklets. Bound to an out-of-the-way home place, she managed to make people come to her; the world, one might say, beat a path to her door.

As for the poetry, there is nothing quite like her homespun variety. People want to say something about their lives and poetry that is not involved with traditional form is a way to do it. Some of the poems in the following pages have not appeared in print before.

W. M. T.

May 1984

Nancy Luce - Her Life

hundred years ago when Nancy Luce published and sold her poems herself, people laughed at them, and at her. In our time, however, her poems appear in a different light. I for one found them intriguing. Written in rough-hewn, ungrammatical language, they reflect a daily existence and way of life that has gone. I felt personality on every page, individuality, inner strength and sometimes, humor.

Who was Nancy Luce? What sort of person had she been? Was anyone left who had seen her, or was I too late for that? I inquired at the public library in her home town, and at the post-office general store. I spoke with older residents in the village. Eventually learning of Gertrude Turner, I called on her at her house on Music Street. Ninety years old, Mrs. Turner said when she was about eight, she had gone with her mother to see Nancy Luce. They had taken her a basket of food for Nancy was one of the poor in the town, and not only poor, but sick and strange. Mrs. Turner said she had been afraid because of the way Nancy looked. She had never forgotten the raggedy half-starved apparition, dimmed eyes beneath lids that had no lashes, a toothless collapsed faced peering out from a tightly kerchiefed head.

Native daughter and lifelong inhabitant of Martha's Vineyard, the triangular island that lies six miles south of the heel of Cape Cod as the herring gull flies, eight as the ferry runs from Woods Hole to Vineyard Haven, Nancy Luce was born August 23, 1814.* At that time the Vineyard, one of the long-settled places in the young republic, was organized into three towns -- town being the New England term for township -- Edgartown, Tisbury and Chilmark, plus an Indian Reservation. As the years passed, the number of towns increased. In 1870 the Reservation became the town of Gay Head. Oak Bluffs separated from Edgartown in 1880 and in 1892 West Tisbury won independence from Tisbury. The census of 1820 counted 3,292 persons in the County of Dukes County (Martha's Vineyard, the Elizabeth Islands and Noman's Land) but did not tally the Indians. It would seem there were about three hundred.

Miss Luce was born on a farm on Tiah's Cove Road

*According to her statement as recorded by Richard L. Pease, Assistant Marshal, who counted "Free Inhabitants in Tisbury" for the 1850 Census.

in the present-day town of West Tisbury. Then, as now, West Tisbury was the Island's farming center but the emphasis then was on sheep. Virtually every farm raised a few, for home use if nothing more, while larger farms raised hundreds. Sheep pastured all over the Vineyard, and on the Elizabeth Islands and Noman's as well. Local lore speaks of hills and bottoms white with sheep. Sheep graze closely and evenly. They are destructive of young shrubs and trees. So the woodlands were less and there must have been less poison ivy; sheep are fond of it.

Tiah's Cove where Nancy's father, Philip Luce, had his farm and homestead is one of the many coves of Tisbury Great Pond. The great ponds that border the Vineyard's south side harbored a number of farming communities -- Pohoganut, Scrubby Neck, Deep Bottom, Quansoo, Quanaimes -- all but their names long since vanished. In addition to his homestead, Philip Luce owned or had an interest in half-a-dozen holdings that included woodland and salt-marsh meadow. The marshes surrounding the ponds furnished an abundance of blackgrass hay, an inferior variety but sheep, and even cattle, managed to survive winters on it. He also had a tract of cultivated grass called English meadow, or English mowing. He owned an earmark for sheep, duly recorded and perhaps inherited from his father -- "a crop in the right ear and two slits in the crop" -- the crop being the ear

11

with the upper part removed. He owned a pew in Tisbury Meeting House.

Philip Luce was forty, his wife Anna Manter Luce, thirty-five, and they had been married three years when Nancy, their only child, arrived. It was not a typical family. The usual pattern in that time and place was to marry young and generate numerous offspring who then became, to a certain extent, the property of the father, or the mother. Many hands were needed to do the work that made a family farm flourish -- able to provide almost all needs for food, clothing, fuel, and shelter; the money for taxes, and necessities not produced on the farm, and a few luxuries. Children were expected to work and hand over their earnings until they came of age; they were essential to the family farm economy. As the only asset of this kind available to her older-than-usual parents, Nancy undoubtedly was as exploited as she later said.

When Nancy walked to school -- late 1820s, early 1830s -- Massachusetts public schools were at a low point. Under a decentralized school district system, free schools, the one-time pride of the Bay Colony, had been in decline for forty years, losing public interest and financial support; while the reforms Horace Mann (1796-1859) would inaugurate lay ahead, just over the horizon. In the Town of Tisbury, for example, the annual school appropriation amounted to less than one dollar per scholar -- as those who attended the one-

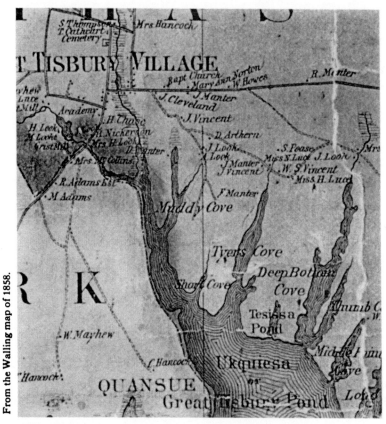

From the Walling map of 1858.

"Miss N. Luce" on the map above Tiah's (Tyers) Cove.

room schools were called. The school term may have been no more than two or three months. Still, at a time when many received no schooling at all -- when illiteracy was common -- Nancy learned to read, work with numbers and most important, to write;

penmanship was highly esteemed. A fine hand was a mark of distinction and Nancy had a flair for the baroque style then in fashion; tradition says it was sometimes taught by sea captains in the intervals between long voyages. In general, however, formal education had little chance to inform or shape her.

Nineteenth-century life was harsh for everyday people; it demanded constant hard work from men -- perhaps even more from women -- and often from children. Sickness and old age were terrible problems. In 1865, then in her 50s, Nancy wrote in a fragment of autobiography, *Sickness Downfalls:*

> "My poor father used to own property enough, he arnt it himself, he owned english meadow in Tisbury, & in West Tisbury. His sickness, & my poor mother's sickness, a number of years, caused him to sell all his english meadow, part his woodland, part his clearland, a great flock of sheep, young cattle, a pair of great oxen, a horse, some cows, &c &c. to get money to pay a number of Doctors, & folks to stay with mother a number of years, most of this when I was a little girl. . . . See what sickness is."

Her parents sick and invaliding, the task of keeping the family afloat fell on her. At nineteen she went to work on her own. The kind of work she undertook -- buying, selling, and bartering -- was unusual. It offered a chance to make a better living. Whose idea was it? Relatives on her mother's side, I would guess. The Manter family, as will appear later, was supportive.

Probably someone saw that a need existed: that the farming enclave around Tiah's Cove could do with an agent to transact business down-Island in Edgartown. Edgartown, the shire town, a whaling port in its heyday, was making money and putting up lovely elegant dwellings. The metropolis of Martha's Vineyard, it was the place where products of the farm, and of home industry, went to be sold or exchanged. But Edgartown was a long way off -- ten miles over roads little more than narrow tracks -- a day's work to go there and back. A capable farm-raised girl who also knew her three r's, Nancy was mentally qualified for such work, and physically too because she could ride. Not many women did -- certainly not many farm women, but Nancy did and loved it. Legend calls her an outstanding horsewoman.

So Nancy carried down-Island to one Timothy Coffin, postmaster and Edgartown merchant, the yarn that she and neighboring women spun, the kersey they wove -- a coarse woolen homespun -- and the stockings and mittens they knitted. She exchanged them for coffee, candles, calico, handkerchiefs, lace, saleratus (bicarbonate of soda), figs, dates, cloves, ginger, tobacco -- to name a few of the articles she mentioned. Candles, one might note, were often made on the farm from tallow and bayberry wax but the candles Nancy brought up-Island were doubtless spermaceti candles -- made right there in Edgartown -- the best source of illumination until kerosene came on the market shortly after the Civil War. The stockings and mittens that Mr. Coffin acquired were sold to whalemen getting ready to sail, or to vessels carrying goods on consignment up and down the coast.

Nancy's enterprise prospered. Now she was able to buy for her own use a four-poster bed with curtains, a blanket, and a bureau with a key to the drawers. Her father's house was very small; she may not have had a separate room so the curtained bed and the locked bureau gave her a little privacy. That was a gain, but best of all, "the cream of it," she wrote later, was the riding she did on those Edgartown expeditions. "You do not know what a site [sight] of good it did me."

She rode, but did she own a horse? I think not. The family could not afford it, nor did they have a place to stable it. Had Nancy owned a horse, she would have written about it, left a record of its name and character, birth and death, for she had a passion for animals.

If she had no horse of her own, then whose horse did she ride? I would say one of her cousin's on the Manter side, or an uncle's; perhaps the same person who had steered her into commerce and trade also furnished the transportation -- on a business basis of course.

Nancy like to ride hard; she wrote that she galloped. Evidently she rode astride -- not side-saddle; that was for women of a different class. I wonder if she had a saddle at all or rode instead on a blanket -- Indian fashion. Then again, if she could borrow a horse, she could borrow a saddle and saddlebags. As to how she dressed herself for riding, apparently not quite as usual. She had some clothes reserved for the purpose -- perhaps a shorter than usual home-made dress, a pair of longer than the usual longish underpants, her own make woolen stockings, and conceivably boughten boots or shoes. With dress and petticoat bunched up fore and aft, she could enjoy the sense of freedom and power that goes with riding well. Much later, tales were told of her prowess. It was said she jumped stone walls and fences.

Young and healthy, mobile and in business for herself, throughout her youth she lived an exceptionally independent life. In spite of an overload of work, and problems with her ailing parents, she got around as few of her female neighbors ever did; most did not see Edgartown oftener than once or twice a year. The oldest village on the Island, and at that time the largest and wealthiest, Edgartown presented a new world to the up-Island girl. Like all New England's great whaling ports, Edgartown had a cosmopolitan, even exotic flavor. Nancy was there when Captain Valentine Pease built his house in 1836. He was the master of the *Acushnet,* the vessel Herman Melville shipped in. She might have seen the giant pagoda tree that stands on South Water Street when it was an infant, brought from China in a pot by Captain Thomas Milton in 1837. One way or another she may have learned that the whaling families considered themselves the aristocrats of the Island, a goodly number of notches higher in the social scale than the farmers.

Her business transacted, there was plenty for Nancy to see before going home to Tiah's Cove -- shipwrights' shops, sail lofts, coopers' and ships chandlers' shops, whaleships fitting out for a voyage to the Pacific Ocean, or a ship just returned from a two, three, or four year voyage. Nancy saw Dr. Daniel Fisher's spermaceti candle factory and, between North Water Street and the harbor, his bakeries for making hardtack.* She may have seen Dr. Fisher himself. Businessman and banker as well as medical man, with an interest in many of Edgartown's whaling fleet, he was the richest man on the Vineyard. Did Nancy ever tread the "Bridge of Sighs," the long wooden walk that led to the Edgartown Lighthouse, where young men walked with young women before the start of a long whaling voyage?

Her records show her in her twenties dealing with Messrs. Munro and Morse, Edgartown, buying dry-goods, groceries, and household wares at a trade discount and selling them up-Island at the retail price. "The price we retail the goods for, you will find on the

*She probably stopped at the marble shop across the street and admired the handsome marble gravestones.

18

Nancy's house as it looks now (1984), front door boarded up.

front part of the bill and the prices we charge you on the opposite side, and we hope they will all come to you in order," the merchants advised her.

In this way Nancy supported herself and her parents until 1840 when at age twenty-six, a great change occurred. She too became sick. In a poem penned many years later she wrote, "First cause of destroying my health, / I drove myself with work over 12 years, / Then I met with the first heart-rendering death. . . ." But what death she referred to has not come to light.

Some have said it was a pet milch goat whose demise she recorded early that year in her Bible. Others have looked for an ill-starred romance but have found no evidence. In December she wrote, "Mr. Munro do excuse me for keeping you out of the pay so long. I have not been able to do much nor see to much. I have been deprived of the enjoyments of coming down. . ."

Cooped up in the smoke-blackened little farmhouse, Nancy turned to time-honored solaces -- painting and writing. Desperate to brighten up her surroundings, she wrote to Edward Munro, September 1842:

> You willing to send me about $3 in tobacco such as will sell quick, if you can let me have it so that I can make as much as 5 cents on a pound or more I will send you the money for it when I sell it. You willing to send me a box of water paints & charge to me one that has gay colors in it bright yellow and light yellow and orange and light red & other gay colors & a brush or two if you have them & if you havnt any brushes send me the box if you are willing. I think it is best for me to try to make a few pictures if I can to take up my mind so that the medicines can have a chance to help if possible. . . . You willing to send me some paper the largest size and clear white but if it is a little on the bluish cast it will do but I want the largest size. Dont let folks know anything about this. . . send me the box as privet as possible. . . ."

Late in October she pleaded with Mr. Munro, "Did you receive a billet from me some time ago asking you to get a box of paints for me. . . & a little brush or two with it. You willing to send me some rice at the amount of 50 cents & charge it to me & I will pay you as soon as posable. Put the paint box in with the rice & then nobody cant know it." She also asked for two "first rate steel pens." Her tone is less than confident -- as though her credit has suffered. But apparently Mr. Munro was willing; in any event he kept her letters that were in effect IOU's.

Through her twenties -- very difficult years for her -- Nancy painted and wrote. None of her paintings have survived. There are, however, the decorations, the idiosyncratic creations with which she embellished fragments of writing and tiny manuscript books. She did not pen these little books in the cursive Spencerian style learned in school, but hand-lettered them, influenced, I suspect, by contemporary wood-block alphabets and typefaces seen in the advertising arts. Whatever the influences, however, her lettering was distinctly her own. Beginning with *Hard Hearts*, 1844, she made the word heart her hallmark; the conventionalized heart of popular culture became her logo. Relationships, she implied, existed heart to heart. The heart, the center of being, stood for the wisdom of feeling as opposed to the wisdom of reason. *Hard Hearts*, thirty-two very small, hand cut, folded and stitched pages, is an irrational account of real or imagined persecutions, nameless maladies, bad luck, and uncontrolled lamenting, but with warm praise for one person -- her doctor.

People are determined that father's property shall be spent, & won't allow me to have any to help myself with. How can they be so hard against me. How much kinder they would be if they would cut my head off, instead of throwing me on the town [supported by poor relief provided by the town]. Do consider, & have reason, & pity.... I want that my folks should have income of their property, to maintain them with victuals, & clothes, and everything comfortable through life & not squandering their property away from their poor hard fortune child.... Do read this with attention and feeling....

Some of my worst complaints are different complaints than people commonly have, they are dreadful to undergo and dangerous.... I have been selling off my things, all this long time, to get money towards paying expenses.

Do consider how hard it is... & cannot earn anything for over four years & confined in this melancholy, & dreadful looking house, & no cleaning done, & no painting done... & 2 old folks come to nothing... & they are unwell & complaining, & lose their reason dreadful fast....

But the worst thing about her illness, whatever it may have been -- worse than loss of income, dirty house and senile parents -- was that it prevented her from riding and getting out and seeing people. She missed going to Edgartown, known as Old Town; and to West Tisbury village called New Town; and to Holmes Hole, the village whose name was changed in 1871 to Vineyard Haven. Telling her story over and over, reiterating her plight and plaint, she hit on two basic poetic devices -- repetition and refrain.

22

You cannot realize how hard it is to me, because I cannot go at New Town. O how hard. & cannot go at Edgartown. O how hard. & cannot go at Holmes Hole. O how hard. & cannot go anywhere. O how hard. . . .

You cannot realize how it hurts my feelings to smell in my drawers, because I used to smell the same smell, when I took out my clothes, to ride somewhere, & now I am deprived of it. O how hard. . . .

It hurts my feelings to see white frosty mornings, or pleasant calm days, because I cannot ride. O how hard. & so it does to smell the sweet air. & so it does to hear the flies buzz. & so it does to hear the birds sing. Because it is so hard to me, because I cannot ride. . .

The doctor who won Nancy's commendation, William H. Luce, was a Vineyard man, the same age as herself. An 1840 graduate of the Medical School of Bowdoin College, he had just completed his course of instruction when he was called to treat Nancy and her father and mother. He lived in the village, two miles from Tiah's Cove, and his clapboard house with outbuilding attached -- his apothecary shop -- is still standing (1984).* If he and Nancy were related, they were distant kinsmen; Luce was the Island's most common surname. Earlier, in 1807, there were said to be forty-one distinct families of Luce on the Vineyard. Nancy wrote about her illness and Dr. Luce in 1845:

Some of these years that I undergo the most, then I cannot do the leastest morsel to a picture, nor write not any, I undergo so much, & some part of the year, when I

*In 1840, the apothecary shop was in a separate building a short distance from Dr. Luce's residence. It was moved and attached to the house in December 1879.

23

feel a little better, then there is only some days, & some part of the day, that I can do a little at a picture, or write a little. . . .

Dr. Luce will do a good deal better for sick people, than any other one else will do, because he is a wonderful patient, & kind person, & skilful, & a wonderful upright person. . . .

Dr. Wm. Luce has cured many complaints for me and helpt many more of them, slowly, and patched along some more of them, all this long time. It seems as if, 2 of my worst complaints cannot be cured, only patched along, & helpt very slowly. Discouraging.

What was Nancy's trouble? Anger? Depression? Migraine? Did Dr. Luce have a name for it? If so, it would seem he did not tell Nancy. If he had, she probably would have announced it somewhere in her chronicles of herself. Those who thought they were physicians, did not hesitate to make pronouncements. "Some people say that I can do better, if I did but think so, & that nothing ails me but nervous mind. . . ," Nancy wrote.

Nervous mind -- going all to pieces with nerves -- was given the name "neurasthenia" a generation later. "In this country nervous exhaustion (neurasthenia) is more common than any other form of nervous disease," wrote George M. Beard (1839-1883). "With the various neuroses to which it is allied, and to which it leads, it constitutes a family of functional disorders that are of comparatively recent development, and that abound especially in the northern and eastern part of the

Dr. Luce's house as it looks now (1984).

United States. . . . It is at once the most frequent, most interesting, and most neglected nervous disease of modern times," he wrote in his pioneering study in nineteenth century psychiatry, *A Practical Treatise on Nervous Exhaustion (Neurasthenia)*, 1880*. Among the causes of neurasthenia -- a catchall word -- Dr. Beard listed worry, work, nervous strain, heredity, climate, and also the social and cultural environment.

Overworked women were a commonplace of the social and cultural environment then and later. Nancy Luce reminds me of women I saw on small stony farms in Maine in the 1920s before rural electrification arrived. Exhausted, nervous, half-crazed, women like

*It is interesting to note that this book was reprinted in 1971.

her were legion and for the most part, silent. What distinguishes Nancy is that she spoke out in her writing:

> It is hard that I used to be confined at home, & was a slave, & maintained my folks for over eleven years. I kept it private all this time, but now I mention it because I'm sarved so bad. I used to buy 3 barrels & a half of flour every year. & over a hundred weight of cheese, every year, that my folks eat. & mutton, & beef in plenty. & part of father's clothes. It amounts to most six hundred dollars, the truth. I used to make double stockings nights, & sold them for money, & give it to my folks. & the income I had for selling, I give my folks.

What a sad affair the Philip Luce farm had become. Even milking the cow was a problem; Nancy no longer had the strength for it while her father did not do it right. I do not suppose he was expected to don clean overalls before milking but a self-respecting person like Nancy would demand that he keep the cow clean, brushed and groomed and free of dust and dried dung, that he scour the milk pail, wash the cow's udder before milking, and his hands, and while milking keep the milk off his hands, and the cow from swishing her tail. Had he done these things his daughter could not have written as she did. "Milk is all the income we have, & besides that I cannot eat anything but milk, without hurting me. . . . When I take milk in my mouth, I cannot help having to puke, when I cannot watch father, & see him milk, & tell him what to do, & what not to do. I suffer with nastiness, I cannot stand

26

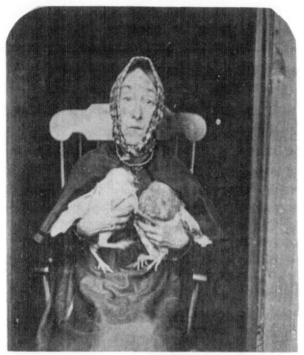

Nancy with bantams. "I want to hold up 2 at a time."

nastiness." Her dependence on milk for sustenance suggests intestinal disorders.

Of various neurasthenic symptoms noted by Dr. Beard, Nancy seems to have suffered from headaches, weak spells, and almost certainly, neuralgia. She was abnormally sensitive to wind, and the winds do blow over Martha's Vineyard. A photograph of her at about forty-five shows an unusually long oval sad-eyed face wrapped in a kerchief. Her features are well formed

27

and large. Her hands are large. Summing up and at the same time begging the question, she wrote, "All that ails me is what I have met with. I am a strong natured person. If I had not been I should [have] been dead, years ago. . . ."

In a countryside where everybody was known, and where there was no place to hide, Nancy's hard-to-define illness, and doubtless erratic behavior, could not go unnoticed:

> People always talk about me cruelly, they always accuse me of almost everything that I am not guilty of. How can they be so hard against me. . . I have not any friends, to speak a kind word to me. . . & nobody to have any kind thoughts about me. & nobody to have any tender feeling for me, & nobody to speak a word to try to help me, no how nor no way. . . ."

Were these grievances real or delusional?

On May 1, 1847, Philip Luce, age seventy-five, died. Five months earlier he had deeded Nancy his "homestead lands together with a house. . . all. . . right and interest in and to a certain tract of meadows land lying at a place called Quansoo Meadows. . . also one cow. . ." Early the next year word got out that two neighboring farmers, William S. Vincent and Jeremiah Manter, would place an article in the town warrant requesting appointment of a guardian for Nancy. Their interest in doing so may or may not have been friendly. In any case, others opposed the idea. Two

28

days before the annual Town Meeting twelve residents petitioned the Honorable Theodore G. Mayhew, Esq., Judge of Probate for the County of Dukes County, saying that Nancy "is in our opinion fully suitable to manage or superintend her own affairs at the present time without the assistance of the Town or from any other source." Many of the petitioners were cousins on Nancy's mother's side. Dr. Luce and his colleague, Dr. J. Y. E. Gage, were also among the signers.

At the Town Meeting, March 20, 1848, held that year in the South Baptist Meeting House, West Tisbury, a majority of the voters instructed the Selectmen to ask the Judge to appoint a guardian and nine days later the Selectmen did so. Citing the two farmer neighbors mentioned above and "others" they said, "Upon a complaint. . . representing that Nancy Luce. . . Single Woman, being in possession of some estate, but through Insanity and imbecility is liable to become chargeable to the Town, we therefore respectfully request your honor to appoint some suitable person as Guardian. . ."

Two weeks later, Dr. Luce filed his own report on Nancy. He wrote Judge Mayhew, "She wishes for me to state to your Hon. that she does not desire to have a guardian placed over her, that she has never applied to the town for assistance, nor does she intend doing so; and humbly requests that you will allow her the privilege of enjoying her property as she pleases. So far as I am acquainted with her, I think her competent to manage her own affairs and to take care of her property."

On July 3, 1848, Judge Mayhew turned down the Selectmen's petition. And the following year, as though begging her pardon, the Town did something for Nancy. At the 1849 annual meeting it was voted that "the Meadows and Beach Tax standing against Nancy Luce be paid by the Town."

Acquitted, so to speak, of imbecility, Nancy managed her house, farm and mother as she saw fit and was able to. Her mother assigned her "all dower rights" in the property and also "seven sheep more or less." Three years later, on June 14, 1851, Anna Manter Luce, seventy-four, died. Nancy was now near thirty-seven. The human members of her family were gone yet she was not entirely alone. She had her little family of livestock and chickens, each named by her, and each a personality.

Free to make her own decisions, Nancy sold some land and put the money into repairing the house. The back room which had its own outside door and thumblatch, stabled the cow. The front room remained a kind of colonial kitchen; Nancy cooked in iron pots hanging from cranes in the walk-in fireplace. Hearth fire was her source of heat and, in the evening, most of the light. Neighbors advised her to get a stove.

Gravestone in West Tisbury Cemetery.

The *Vineyard Gazette* by this time was carrying advertisements for several makes. A stove producing more heat from less fuel would have made sense and been more convenient. Nancy replied with a squib titled "Stove":

They abuse me to spend everything in stove, & wood to
set by, I wont, I need other things hundred times more.
Wood wont warm me in winter, nor strengthen me, milk

porridge will warm me, & strengthen me too.

In a similar vein she penned "Wood They Think Is a Doctor":

> When I tell folks about being sick some of them say, you must have some wood, there see, as if wood skillful Doctor, to cure dangerous complaints, and some say did you get some cold, &c &c. See how much they believe.

In her thirties Nancy seemed to improve. She took up knitting again, made butter, did a little trading, but she could hardly walk. She was bound by her house, her front and back yards. She almost certainly kept on writing, following up *Hard Hearts* with more hand-printed booklets. Those floriated handcrafted little books, of which a few specimens survive,* could hardly have brought in any money but probably adumbrated the mechanized job-printed booklets to come.

On February 25, 1857, she sent Dr. Luce some mittens with a letter concealed in them:

> This is all the way I could send you a letter in these mittens. Now if you take the advantage of me & wont send me anything, because I no friends, it is a cruel wicked thing. My health is worse again, I feel miserbly & dont feel able to do the leastest thing, but forced to do something, everything I do hurts me, the more I stur, & stand up & walk, the more misery I am in. You like to take this 3 pair of mittens & send me portwine to take inside, & brandy to bathe my bowels. I bought the mittens. If you send it, send it quick, by anyone you can,

*Three from the Dukes County Historical Society Archives are reproduced in the Appendix.

32

Nancy in her last years in her house.

tell them it is something you fixed for me, if you send it by my relation, make them think it is dreadful stuf, or they will pore out half of it & put in water. Send it by anyone you can or send it by them that brings this. I was forced last fall to send to another Doctor & get medicines, for I should been down sick, because you are so hard against me. Dont let it be known that I was forced to send to another Doctor. If you dont like to send me something for these mittens, you may give me credit for them & keep me in misery till I die. I am dreadful weak across me, & lame, & other miserable feelings, puts me in misery to stur. I have hard pain in both sides great part of my time. & hard pain in my stomach by spels, it is not rhumatisum. I have 3 sorts of rhumatism, I am not telling you about that now. I have cutting pain in my bowels mornings, that is weakness. I have the torment often. that pain in my head I have undergone such a site with all this time is some better. . . I dont have so much of it & not so severe but the headache is full as bad. I have hard headache undergo a great deal with it, when I have it hard it takes away all the strength across me. I have a number of poor feelings all over me besides these. Will you call in the first time you come this way, I won't stop [keep] you. Them symtoms of consumtion are as bad as they have been, it hurts my stomach to talk very bad, but I must talk, but when I have spells I cant scarsly speak, it seems as if my breath was most spent then I cant talk, the cough is as bad as ever, that hoursness rises bad in my stomach, when I go to bed nights. My heart aches for them dear little hearts, befear I shall die & leave them to suffer & be bulyed.

Do excuse me about them stockings I promised you to give credit for, I havnt been able to knit. if I get able to knit you shall have them, I want to knit dreadfuly. I havnt been able to knit scarsly any for more than a year & half, on the acount of pain in my head & other misery. . . .

If you have any coots to sell this spring you like to sell me once in while one fat coot all ready dresed, & take a pair of blue mixed stockings in May, if I cant get able to knit them I will buy them for you. the cow will be dry in April & then I need the coots to make broth on. If you have some now to spare I like to have some whenever you have them to sell.

34

> Do try to understand all my writing it is hard work for
> me to write.

Was Nancy's an aggravated case, or was she simply more vocal than most? The golden age of patent medicines must have been speaking to common ailments. Advertisements appearing each week in the *Vineyard Gazette* may not have helped the afflicted much, but probably aided the paper's financial health. Week after week, one Professor Holloway proclaimed in the columns of the four-page *Gazette* that "Holloway's Pills are the best remedy known in the world for the following diseases: Ague, Asthma, Bilious Complaints, Blotches on the Skin, Bowel Complaints, Colics, Constipation of the Bowels, Consumption, Debility, Dropsy, Erysipelas, Female Irregularities, Fevers of all kinds, Fits, Gout, Headache, Indigestion, Inflammation, Jaundice, Liver Complaints, Lumbago, Piles, Rheumatism, Retention of Urine, Scrofula, or King's Evil, Sore Throats, Stone and Gravel, Secondary Symptoms, Tic Douloureux, Tumours, Ulcers, Venereal Affections, Worms, of all kinds, Weakness from whatever cause, &c., &c.," -- a list perhaps comprehensive enough to embrace all Nancy's troubles. Davis's Vegetable Pain Killer, manufactured on the Vineyard, alleviated pain with opium. Most nostrums, however, relied on alcohol. Which is what Dr. Luce seems to have done. But he also had another palliative in his armamentarium --

kindness. He was kind to Nancy.

Early in 1858 -- the middle of a February night -- Ada Queetie, one of the dear little hearts Nancy spoke of in her letter to Dr. Luce, passed away. One must try to imagine the scene, the death of that close companion, a small aging hen, to the lonely woman on Tiah's Cove Road. When Beauty Linna died the next year, the stage was set for the writing of *Poor Little Hearts.*

I have said West Tisbury was the Island's farming center. It was also the scene of the Martha's Vineyard Agricultural Society's annual Fair, an August occurrence in our time, but originally a harvest-moon event. On the eve of the Fair, October 25, 1858, Dr. Luce wrote Nancy, "... in regard to your cow -- I have done my best to dispose of your cow but without success. ... The only chance I see for you now is to send your cow up to the fair tomorrow and sell her for what she will fetch if it is no more than $5.00 -- & I will get up a subscription paper and try to get money enough to buy you another -- young and good if possible -- I have no doubt but what I can raise it... will do all I can for you."

Acting on doctor's orders -- accepting the necessity for doing so -- the reason being that the cow was dry, no longer giving milk and too old to breed again, Nancy sent her to the Fair to be sold. But what feelings of guilt the decision must have cost. Send an old cow away? She was not an anonymous animal but a name,

Postcard published by J. N. Chamberlain, Oak Bluffs.

a housemate, and member of the family. Just the same, her time had come; the old cow departed, and Dr. Luce having raised the money, or put it up himself, a new cow arrived on Tiah's Cove Road. These events moved Nancy to write,

> Poor Sarah Wilbor must be hurled a way off,
> In the 15th year and a half of her age,
> Only I did do it,
> She always behaved well with me,
> And always minded all I said to her,
> She was carried off the 27th of October,
> Susannah Allen was brought the 16th of November 1858

Whoever selected Susannah Allen was a good judge of a heifer -- a cow less than three years old and that has freshened (given birth and come into milk) only

37

once. In August 1860, Nancy sent Dr. Luce a running scroll twenty-five inches long.

I write you this letter about the cow, she is a cow; how could I have such a good cow; how could I have such good luck, I am [a] good deal more pleased with her than I was with the others, she is the best cow that ever was owned here, by me or anyone else. She is firstrate on every account, good for milk, good for butter, gives richer milk than the old cow did & she give good milk, folks said. . . the heifer give better. . . when the weather is cool enough the cream rises thick hard yellow, I take it off and let it stand overnight & mash it into butter with a iron spoon in less than one minute. . . . She is the gentlest cow I ever knew, & the nicest cow I ever knew, O you dont know how nice she is to come to be milked. When I first had her she was sure to lift up her head from the grass at the first word as quick as I spoke her name, & come as fast as she could walk & make no stop, & in the house & stand still to be milked, now she comes before I ask her, she has done this great while, she comes before I want to milk & puts her nose to the doorlatch & there she keeps it till I let her in & milk, & then she goes to her nights lodging. how could I have such good luck to have a nice cow, to come so nice to be milked, she milks the easyest I ever knew any cow, I bring out the milk by wholesales. . . . If I could had any cow on the island that I had a mind to, I dont believe I could got one that would done so well in my situation, as this one. . . . I hope this cow will last me as long as I live, she is so good on every account. She is neat looking. goodnatured. She has grown larger, & fater this summer. . . .

Folks run off with all my new milk & butter, hogback,

38

& wont pay me anything that I can pay my expenses with, Now if I dont have some resolution, I am ashore & cant get along. They ought to consider that my fall expenses must be accomplished & must be payed this fall. I must have 1000 of good topstalks, & as many more as I can get. I must have 5 or 6 bushels of corn, & not get catched with nothing for poor hens to eat. The hay must be saved.... I owe some debts in the neighbourhood, must be payed this fall. I must have a little wood for winter, I shall let myself be cold, but I must have a little. I must have meal to thicken milk with. & taxes. & other expenses. If I could sold milk this summer when it was poor butter weather, I could got along firstrate about paying my expenses. I have had more milk this summer than I have had any summer, for a number of summers. I have offered milk for sale all summer. My work folks [people who did work for her] had milk & butter of me, I payed them all I owed them. Every time it come up splendid butter weather then all the folks that want milk, come raven after it & when one comes after all the rest have got it all, that one goes & calls me ugly, because they cant have more milk than the cow gives. They all after it, because it is splendid butter weather, & when hot & cant make butter, they wont touch it. They do so, so that I shant have anything to help myself with. this cow's milk keeps well. Now folks have asked me to sell them milk this fall, I answered them & said, you may buy milk this fall where you bought it this summer, when hot & I could not make butter, & offered milk for sale. I am thankful this cow is good for butter. I wont be so imposed on. Now I am giving out word I shant let any more new milk go when it is splendid butter weather. But when poor butter weather I will sell new milk for money, I will sell skim milk for price according. Now all the folks that wants butter comes raven on me after all my butter, part of them say you got any butter I must have all you have got, I must have it, I must have it, I must have all you got, I will work for you some time another, & rest of them say you got any butter, I want you should let me have it all, I will work for you some time another, & when I am in haste to have work done, they wont do it. Now if they want butter, they may have it, but they must pay money for it, as they do other places, I hear, & know. The traders will take my butter, & pay my expenses.

Some fancy pen work adorned this letter and Nancy added two postscripts. Squeezed into the space at the bottom of the last page, opposite her large and elaborate signature, she wrote, "I like for you to keep this letter to remember me by if you please. Let folks read it."

Let folks read it -- let them know what is going on behind the pleasant-seeming facade of rural and village life. Nancy insists on being heard. And like the general run of writers, she hopes and wants to leave a trace. Dr. Luce kept the letter, his son after him, and then his grandson. It is now in the Archives of the Dukes County Historical Society in Edgartown, together with other letters from Nancy.

The second postscript pertained to Susannah Allen. "Where is a likely place to have my cow led to in November, to calve the August following," she asked her doctor. Susannah Allen, incidentally, must have

A rare picture of Nancy -- and Jersey cow?

been a Jersey, the ideal family cow -- small, trim, good-looking, gentle, a producer of milk rich in butterfat, and not a big eater.

As for what Nancy herself ate, she dined pretty much on the same as her chickens -- milk and grain. A note from her to a Captain George Luce was given me by his great granddaughter, Alice Mayhew Davies Mathewson. Penned on a 2 x 5 scrap of paper, dated May 1860, it reads, "Cpt. George Luce, You like to send me a bushel of good yellow southern Corn meal to make porridge on, & for chickens to eat too. & a little cheap flour to make breakfast porridge on, & charge it it me, I will pay you the money, as soon as I can get the money & can get a chance to send it safe to you. If you cant get a chance to send it straight to me, you may send it in Town & leave it with some of my folks. Nancy Luce"

At forty-six, Nancy, though sick, was in her creative prime. In September she had another important matter to consult Dr. Luce about. She was writing *Poor Little Hearts,* giving thought to the spelling of names dear to her, and how their pronunciation might be affected by local characteristics of speech. She knew most Vineyarders pronounced Tiah's, Tyer's; Martha's as if spelled Mather's. She wrote the doctor:

> You willing to be so kind as to let me know how to spell the names of my poor deceased friends. . . how to spell them to be on sure grounds to always have them sounded out on a, just as I used to speak them, if I put a to the end of their names as I used to do, they will sound them on r, that must not be. I used to spell them Ada Queta, Beauty Lina, now I spell them Ady Queety. Beauty Linny. I ain't suited yet, to spell them right, to have them sounded on a. If you know, do be so kind as to write them to me on this paper.

Replying on the same sheet, Dr. Luce wrote, "If you wish to sound the a *long* you must put the mark over it so -- ā -- that indicated that it is sounded as in day bay etc. & not like r -- as in short a. Or you can add the y or -- ie -- is very fashionable now as -- Addie Queetie, Beautie Linnie, the ie here sounds like long e --"

Satisfied with the doctor's phonetic prescription,

42

Nancy tried to get her manuscript to a printer, off-Island it would seem -- probably someone in New Bedford -- only to have it returned months later. A letter from a certain Shubael Davis* of West Tisbury, July 28, 1861, informed her, "I regret that I have not forwarded your book before. I hope you will pardon me. I am sorry to say that I did not get your book printed. I saw the printer but he was so bussey he could not attend to it. It was at the commenceing of the war when I saw him and he had a great many extrays to print." The opening shots of the Civil War had been fired the preceding April.

The book would have to wait out the war; years would pass before the printer got to it. During that time she seems to have added only two poems, "Sickness," and "1866." Her days were all taken up with the mechanics of living, care and feeding of cow, hens, and self, and finding money to pay her bills. The everlasting battles with neighbors continued. Nancy wanted hay from the cultivated meadows. She knew the cow would do better on it than on the Quansoo salt-marsh hay, but she had no way of making it. To hire it done would not have paid. She wanted someone to make it on shares, on a lay, as she called it, but no one, apparently, was willing. In May 1862, with haying

*The 1860 Census lists Shubael Davis as a cooper in West Tisbury. He may have made regular trips to New Bedford on business and thus could have offered to help Nancy find a printer. All but the last edition of her poems were printed in New Bedford.

time coming up, she wrote:

> Human, I am tried with them. They keep fighting me
> year after year to stop me from making meadow, keep
> telling me not to make meadow, cost me a good deal. . .
> then they told me not to keep cow, that sot me most
> distracted, cow that I cannot live without, impossible. . . .
> I want to make enough so that I can let it out on a lay,
> & have good hay enough to keep a cow, & sell the
> quansoo hay standing. Consider what a help that would
> be to me. folks keep fighting me yet, to stop me from
> making meadow. They have got my pin feathers up, I
> won't mind them no more. Nancy Luce.
> Dr. Luce & Mrs. Luce, I want you should please to keep
> this letter to remember me by, & let folks read it.

Determination to express herself was not Nancy's only motive for having her poems printed. She saw economic opportunity in them. They were merchandise, something she could sell. Her book might even pay off her debts. But while the book was being held up, what else could she offer? Eggs. She would need more of them, however. She would need to increase production. Very knowledgeable concerning chickens, and ingenious as well, she devised an unusual arrangement for looking after them. Personally, I have farmed, kept hens, and worked with farmers, but never saw or heard of a chicken house like Nancy's. Under the floor in the southeast corner of the back room where the cow resided, she had a circular hole dug, about eight feet in diameter, and five feet deep. Lined with brick, it was nice and dry since

44

Drawing by Norma E. H. Bridwell

Artist's interpretation of Nancy's subterranean chicken house, her "South America."

the soil along Tiah's Cove Road is sandy. The door on the east side of the house allowed light to shine down into it when the trap door was raised at daybreak; long hours of light encourage hens to eat and drink. Several years earlier, Nancy had written the *Vineyard Gazette*, "Mr. Editor. I send you a piece for you to put in your paper if you please, without charging it to me. My pullets commenced laying four months of age. . . . Be good to your hens and not cruel. Consider how you would feel if you could not help yourselves, and folks was cruel to you and let you suffer. I have kept about 8 hens which layed rising 1500 eggs a year. Nancy Luce."

Eggs at four months is a precocious achievement, and almost two hundred per bird per year outstanding for a home flock in those days. What was the secret? "Hens must have clean victuals and clean water to drink," she wrote later. "Take the chill off the water in winter. Keep good yellow southern corn standing by them. . . Give them boiled oats. . . I give my hens boiled oats all the time. . . and sometimes I give them boiled potatoes. I mash it with cream for them. . . . Good flour bread is splendid to make them lay eggs, but I am not able to cook it for them. . . . Keep fine clam shells by them, and gravel sand. . . . Take up the dressing every morning certain. . . Be clever to them. They must not be affrighted. They can never get over it. . . ."

On 1 December 1865, under the rubric "Will you be so kind as to let folks read this letter," Nancy wrote about her underground hen house.*

Now I have me a seller after so long a trial, it was finished 14th day of October 1865. It does me a lovely site of good, now my same old hens lay firstrate, & I keep a few more now. I didnt used to have but a very few eggs at this time of the year, because I was forced to turn them out mornings in the cold & got cut up in the cold, now I keep them in till 9 or 10 oclock, & if to cold then, not let them out till warmer day. the colder it is, the more pleased my hens with my South America, they come in & go down. It is great profit to me. And now I take care my hens with pleasure, so little work, it used to hurt me, it was so hard to take care of them in that way, as it used to be. And I have a place under the stairs to keep things from frost, I didnt used to have anywhere.

Some folks was against my having a seller, because they didnt like I should have anything to help myself with, And they didnt believe how it hurt me to take care of my hens in that way. And they didnt believe how miserable my health. And they didnt care how much poor hens suffered with cold. They need the love of God in their hearts.

My hens used to suffer with heat summer nights, mouth open, wings out from them, panting, it hurt them about laying. Now they can be comfortable both winter & summer.

At the end of the letter she brought up the question of her still-unpublished book.

*The letter was probably to Dr. Luce, although his name is not on it.

> My Book must be printed to pay over $70 I owe for
> foder, taxes, wood, workfolks.... And I must have
> money out [of] my Books to shingle part the house. And
> make meadow. And gravestones & gravefence....

Gravestones and gravefence. Nancy wanted to make a burial ground for certain departed close friends.* Some time later -- probably after her book came forth and her finances, perhaps, improved -- she laid out a graveyard for three greatly loved hens adjoining the east end of her house and surrounded it with a picket fence. Later on she had the fence strengthened, raised, and topped with spikes, business end up, to ward off invaders. Though all trace of the fence and cemetery has vanished, two marble slabs erected to these favorites, and representing a considerable outlay in stonecutting, eventually reached the Dukes County Historical Society where they mystify the new generations of tourists.

Eventually, on a day in 1867 or '68, *Poor Little Hearts* came off the press. A book to Nancy, to the world it was only a sixteen-page pamphlet, 9x5 inches in size, bound in a plain-looking buff paper cover that bore no author's name but only the title in large nineteenth-century wood type, the words stacked one above the other and framed in a simple border. There was of course no publisher's imprint, Nancy being her

---

*At the time Nancy wrote this letter, 1865, Ada Queetie (1858) and Beauty Linna (1859) had died. The third hen buried under a stone, Tweedle Tedel Bebbee Pinky, died in 1871.

Nancy's "gravestones & gravefence" for hens.

own publisher, nor did the print shop attach its name. Oddly enough, the original date on the manuscript, 1860, was retained on the title page -- a nice bibliographical anomaly.

Since no copyright was claimed and no copy deposited with the Library of Congress, *Poor Little Hearts* is not included in the national collection. How many copies were printed? Enough, one might say, to survive and no more. A sizeable number of the first edition seems to have been lost in transit. On September 26, 1868, Nancy drafted a letter to one Samuel Flanders saying,

You must see to this business. You must make good all damage. I am not able in neither body, nor property, to lose that 200 Books. I have a costly house to repair, and fence to get up, and back debts to pay. I keep paying back debts, and forced to pay out a great deal to get chores done. I am dreadful in debt now. I did not ask your son to carry the 200 Books. He asked me. . . .*

Copies of the original edition of *Poor Little Hearts* are exceedingly rare; I have seen only two -- one in the Harris Collection of American Poetry at Brown University, the other in the Dukes County Historical Society Archives.**

In addition to the long title poem, the little first edition published three shorter poems, "1866," "No Comfort," and "Sickness," plus three eccentric notes -- on pork and lard which, unlike her neighbors, Nancy loathed; on her favorite food, milk; and on the fate of her parents. A revised and muted account of the underground hen house came next and finally a catalog, "Hen's Names."

Many authors have printed at their own expense only to find the problem was how to dispose of the product. Experienced in business, Nancy may have asked herself who would buy her poems. The same people who took her milk, butter, and eggs? Not likely.

*Samuel Flanders was well known, having been Keeper of Gay Head Light for years. One of his sons was a mariner and may have offered to "carry the 200 books" from the New Bedford printer to West Tisbury, losing them en route.

**In 1969, the Dukes County Historical Society reprinted *Poor Little Hearts* exactly as originally published.

50

But there was another possible market, namely, the summer visitors. The evangelical fervor that swept the country in the early part of the nineteenth century, hit Martha's Vineyard hard. Camp meetings had been held down-Island since 1835. Baptists and Methodists rather than Congregationalists, the Vineyard's long established church, took the lead in making converts and saving souls. Before long the Methodist Wesleyan Grove Camp Meeting in the present-day town of Oak Bluffs blossomed into the foremost thing of its kind. By 1860, when Nancy first sent *Poor Little Hearts* to the printer, its camp meeting tents had begun to give way to cottages.

Five years passed. The Civil War ended. The postwar boom began. The Oak Bluffs Land and Wharf Company laid out a secular real estate development. The Martha's Vineyard Railroad puffed and chugged from Oak Bluffs to Edgartown to the South Beach at Katama, while the Baptists got up their own camp meeting on the Highlands near the East Chop Light. Back at the Methodist Wesleyan Grove, increasing traffic over the roots of the trees caused the trees to die. A mammoth tent was set up to provide shade. By 1875 the Island's first summer colony, Cottage City, was born and named.

On this sea of enterprise Nancy launched *Poor Little Hearts*, probably in 1868. Visitors from off-Island -- "foreign folk," Nancy called them -- bought it. It aroused curiosity as to its author; poor little hearts were chickens, weren't they? What did the woman who wrote about chickens look like? Here was another opportunity. Nancy had her picture taken and sold it with her book. Photographs were all the rage; the photographers of the Civil War had popularized the new medium. Let me say here as well as anywhere else I believe there were always some persons friendly to Nancy. Though the *Vineyard Gazette* was "only one dollar per year in advance," I do not imagine Nancy subscribing; a dollar was hard to come by. More likely someone passed on the weekly to her. Nancy saw that Charles H. Shute was a persistent advertiser. "Chas. H. Shute & Son. PHOTOGRAPHERS, No. 22 1-2 Main Street, Are prepared to make PHOTOGRAPHS from the smallest size to the largest. Tin Types from the smallest to the 4 4 size.We pay particular attention to copying Pictures, which can be enlarged to any size. And we warrant all our work to be AS GOOD AS CAN BE HAD in this or any other country.... We cordially invite all to come and see our Pictures at the Door, and in the Reception Room."

Since Nancy could not get to Edgartown, she asked Mr. Shute to come to West Tisbury. On November 24, 1858 she wrote,

> I want my hens pictures made. . . folks been asking me to
> have them made. Now if you will come first weekday in
> the forenoon that the weather is good to the front door, I
> will do the best I can if I no sicker. I want to hold up 2 at a

Autography with hearts.

time twice, and hold up one once, she is heavy, others
small, and I want you should make cow, and house, and
myself, and hens, once, that will be 4 pictures. . . . As
soon as I can sell them I will send you your money. . . . I
will keep my hens in my cellar till you come, every
forenoon in weather [that] will do to make them, till 12
o'clock, then let them out. . . .

Exploiting her peculiarities, selling images of herself -- book or photograph twenty-five cents -- Nancy sought to pay her way.

Under "Local Jottings," the *Vineyard Gazette* of July 8, 1870 reported "Miss Nancy Luce received many callers on the 4th, and everything went on smoothly. Last 'Independent' day she was much annoyed by parties who were meddlesome and noisy; so this year she called in the aid of the constable of West Tisbury district, who peremptorily checked any attempt at riot. The bland and courteous officer also acted as usher and escorted the company into the best room."

In September she wrote the *Gazette*, "I am a doctor for hens. I shall have a book printed in the spring if I live, and nothing happens to hender me." Nothing did. She was fifty-six years old.

Sometime in 1871, she brought out *A Complete Edition of the Works of Nancy Luce, of West Tisbury, Dukes County, Mass., Containing "God's Words;" "Sickness;" "Poor Little Hearts;" "Milk;" "No Comfort;" "Prayers;" "Our Saviour's Golden Rule;" and "Hens Names."* Sixteen pages printed on cheap paper by a New Bedford printing house, Fessenden & Baker, *A Complete Edition* revised almost everything in *Poor Little Hearts* -- all, it seems to me, for the worse. The title poem, reworked, appears with its urgency blurred, its passion diluted. A new poem, "Death," not listed on the cover, extolled Tweedle Tedel Bebbee Pinky, the successor to Ada Queetie and

Beauty Linna. Also not listed is a four-page essay, "Doctoring Hens."

> If the will of God could be done in full, it would be a great happiness among dumb creatures and human too.... Be kind to poor hens in every way, and not let them suffer with hunger nor cold; cruelty not in any way; must not affrighten them; doctor them when they have diseases....

A subsequent printing with four pages added, though still dated 1871, came out in 1872.

One neighbor for sure (and there may have been others) took Nancy's books and photos in trade. On August 17, 1871, she wrote,

> Mr. Whiting, Now in this letter I send you 4 Photographs, your daughter wanted them towards the hay, she come last fall after them, I'had none, she got 4 books then towards the hay I owe you for, them 4 books $1, these 4 Photographs $1, that makes $2, I have paid you towards the hay. Please let me know how much more I owe you, and I will pay you, I am dreadful jamed yet with debts, and expenses.... Do excuse me for keeping you out of your pay so long, I been forced to lay out over two hundreds of dollars only on the outside of the house, or the wind would tore it to bits. I am forced to pay about $25 a year for cow's victuals... and about $20 a year to get work done in the house and out, and other expenses &c &c. Do excuse me, poor I sick.

For the "I" Nancy drew a thick block letter with a heart, her logo, in it. Poor heart I sick? Poor I heartsick? Henry L. Whiting, geographer, scientist, and head of U. S. Coastal and Geodetic Survey for

New England, had bought a large farm in West Tisbury in 1852.

An up-and-coming person in town and friend to Nancy was William J. Rotch, a young Justice of the Peace and proprietor of a grain and general store whose place of business stood on the Edgartown Road a short piece east of Dr. Luce's house. Squire Rotch's books show that in the 1870s Nancy bought modest amounts of middlings -- a byproduct of flour milling used as an animal feed -- meal, corn, sugar, molasses, oil, lye and rope; and that she paid for her purchases sometimes in cash, sometimes in chickens which she doubtless knew how to kill humanely and dress.

When President Grant visited Cottage City, 1875, and larger than usual crowds were expected, Nancy reissued *A Complete Edition* in different format, smaller pages and more of them -- thirty-six now. Mercury Job Press, New Bedford, was the printer.*

The additional pages contained Nancy's adaptations from familiar texts stressing salvation, an attempt perhaps to appeal to the customers from Wesleyan Grove. Writing lugubrious verse was much in vogue in that generally credulous age. Nancy, full of evangelical zeal with perhaps a dash of opportunism in it, contributed -- alas -- her share.

I have seen copies of this printing with portrait photographs pasted in and autographing added, a

*The 1875 edition includes the lines that are carved on the gravestones of her dear hearts suggesting that the stones may have been raised in 1874.

From the letter to Henry L. Whiting, August 17, 1871. Nancy's handwriting is not as good as in earlier years.

veritable author's edition. The main change in the text, beyond the new material, was that "Doctoring Hens" has burgeoned into "Hens -- Their Diseases and Cure" with a new introduction.

> Human, do understand how to raise up sick hens to health. Some folks do not know how to doctor hens, they doctor them wrong, it hurts them, and it is dreadful cruel to let them die. It is as distressing to dumb creatures to undergo sickness, and death, as it is for human, and as distressing to be crueled, and as distressing to suffer.

57

> God requires human to take good care of dumb
> creatures, and be kind to them, or not keep any. Now
> do understand, and I will tell you exact.

Instructions for treating various ailments follow but the key to it all is feeling; feeling was her daily bread of the spirit. "Do by dumb creatures as you would wish to be done by if you was dumb creatures. . . ." Nancy tells what to do if hens have "Stoppage in Stomach," "Gapes," "Froth in Throat," "Bag Stone," "Warped Neck," "Swelled Head," et cetera -- her own remedies; or "Lice," a consequence of unclean hen houses and common cause of losses. She not only cared more but really knew more about domestic fowl than the great indifferent majority. Characteristically, she worked random paragraphs into the text, one designated "Cows," another, "Birds," pleasingly haphazard variations on the theme of feeling.

> When I step down to the door, the little harmless birds
> come fly down on the ground, only one yard off my feet,
> and some of them half a yard off my feet. I give them oats
> and dough to eat: they eat it. Will they come to anyone
> else? so few folks have feeling.

James A. Scott, Printer, Cottage City, ran off the final printing. It came out in 1888, two years before Nancy died. All told hundreds -- possibly thousands -- of copies were made but today it is hard to find one.

By the 1870s Nancy had carved out a place for herself in the summer trade; she became a sight on the sightseers' circuit. Livery drivers with rubberneck wagons for hire had long been a part of the Camp

58

Snapshots taken in early 1900s. Graveyard for hens has disappeared; a tombstone has become a doorstop.

Grounds scene, hauling parties from Cottage City to points of interest up-Island. When the fares were ready the drivers would amble across the plains to show off the poet and doctor for hens in her West Tisbury habitat. Arrived in her dooryard without prearrangement, the visitors, after paying to make the trip, felt entitled to look her over, her cow, her hens, and especially the graveyard. Some "behaved well and bought books of me," Nancy wrote. Others laughed at her. "Gross sinners," she called them, and "stone hearts." She was also a stopover for excursionists on their way to Gay Head.

Nancy had also become a target for jokers. The fact that she could not tolerate noise inspired exuberant groups coming from or bound for the Agricultural

Fair to treat her to a shivaree, a serenade with pots and pans. After the 1867 Fair she informed readers of the *Gazette,*

> some hard hearts come with band of music, and sot it going to my door, to murder me alive... they put my head in a dreadful condition. I did not get over it for a number of weeks, and they beat me entirely out. Some of them been telling ever since, they scared me, with the music, that is false, they did not scare me, not one mite, they crueled me in my sickness.

In September 1870 — Fair time again — she wrote the paper, "Lie going three years. Some folks keep telling all about the band scared me... they did not scare me, not one mite, they abused me dreadfully..." Two months later, December 9, 1870, another letter concerning the incident appeared in the Gazette. "Why cannot the young people who visit this sad, eccentric invalid give themselves the happiness to smoothe, instead of setting thorns in her rough way? My pretty damsels, glorious in modern chignons, curled waterfalls, crimps, flounces, and high heels -- did it ever occur to you that with the same weight of years, cares, shattered hopes, and 'long sickness,' your buoyancy would be lost; and you, too, might dwell under shadows quite as deep?"

This comment was signed Pro Bono Publico and written by the grandmother of Ben C. Clough (1888-1975). A Vineyarder and Professor of Classics at Brown University, Mr. Clough played a key role in preserving Nancy's papers.

In the twenty years that remained to Nancy she became the most widely known Vineyarder of her time. Hundreds of picture postcards of her were sold for which she received not a penny. Souvenir booklets of the period showed a view of her house. Describing her as "a singular creature," her writing "a dreary waste of nonsense," *A Guide to Martha's Vineyard and Nantucket*, published in Boston in 1878, gave her the same amount of space it assigned to the lighthouse and cliffs of Gay Head -- two full pages. Did this growing celebrity help the sale of her poems? Did it bring her some inner satisfaction? It won her sympathetic attention, and also the opposite kind. Youthful trangressors continued to harass her. They desecrated the graveyard, banged boards, and one, she wrote, "brought in cow dressing and put it in my entry and shut the door against it. I started them with the lash then. They are awful wicked. Everybody ought to do as they wish to be done by." The lash -- a whip from her riding days? -- and her tongue were her defenses. There was no help close by. She lived on an isolated stretch of road, woods on one side, a bend in the road on the other that hid her from houses farther along. On January 24, 1876, Nancy wrote Dr. Luce:

Can you do anything to stop them schoolboys. . . . I sent to Esq. Rotch the same time, they not stopt, a man told the other day he saw two of them around my house trying to get in about 2 or 3 weeks ago, they was sly then, I did not see nor hear them, I cannot live so, they keep weakening my things. . . and they keep weakening my doors and windows, they will be down, and these damages they destroy my health. . . . It is dreadful dreadful barbarous barbarous, to do me such damages, and make me undergo sickness too, and I expect they will destroy my cow, she is heavy with calf. I cannot live so, what can be done to stop them. . . .

Three years later, April 15, 1879, she wrote Justice of the Peace Jeremiah Pease, naming names of those who vandalized her. "If you think best to call on me," she said, "come and bring my letter, then I can tell you it is my own handwriting and my own composeing. I cannot call on you, impossible. I cannot ride one mite. I cannot walk but a very few yards from my door. . . ." Then a postscript,

Now since I wrote this letter, Sunday 27th, two young men come from Edgartown. I fastend them out, I told them go away, I won't let you in. One of them told me, dam you, then he said, God dam you, that was the words he said to me, then he tried to brake my bolts to my door. You keep him away. I am forced to write this letter not able to write, I sick, and murdered alive.*

Bad as this was, worse was to come. In October 1882, someone roughed Nancy up, "wounded me where my liver is. . . and wounded me back of my right side," she wrote Dr. Luce. She thought it was the same person from Edgartown who had cursed her out several years before.

*In the body of the letter she wrote: "You must **not** stop foreign folks that come from Campmeeting week days and behave well, and bought books of me, I cannot live nor get along without them to come and buy books of me, and behave . . . I cannot live nor get along in this world without selling books."

62

Between 1881 and 1884 *The Cottage City Star,* one of the half dozen and more newspapers that came and went on Martha's Vineyard, reported Nancy sick or harassed, or both, again and again. Her persecutors seem to have been Island people, a certain element that usually did its work at Fair time. But Fair time was a profitable time for her. *The Star* of October 26, 1882, reported that "during the last day of the Agricultural Fair twenty carriage loads of people visited her. Some of them carried their fun a little too far by such acts as shutting their hostess in a closet, etc., but they made up with her by purchasing a large number of her books."

Year after year she struggled to keep from going on the town, and she succeeded. In consideration of all she owed Dr. Luce, she had on June 13, 1871, turned over to him for the sum of $159.45 her property "containing about fifteen acres, more or less, it being my present homestead. Also a certain tract of Meadow in Chilmark...." The arrangement allowed her to occupy it while he paid the taxes though she, apparently, was responsible for the upkeep.*

She tried repeatedly to get him to promise in writing to maintain her beloved hens' graves and, when the time came, have her buried beside them. But the doctor, who had put up with much, seems to have declined these extramedical entreaties. Increasingly

*Although signed by Nancy on June 13, 1871, the sales agreement was not entered in the Dukes County Court House records until December 18, 1873.

ADA QUEETIE
Died Feb. 25, 1858:
Aged most 9 years.

BEAUTY LINNA
Died Jan. 18, 1859:
Aged over 12 years.

Gravestones that can be hard to understand unless you know Nancy.

she complained to him, seemed to feel that he was neglecting her. The doctor as well as the patient was getting older. In the end he survived her by only a year.

Meanwhile her back room no longer housed a well-bred critter like Susannah Allen. Instead, Nancy coped with a half-wild scrub, the bellowing cow with unsymmetric udder that she named Red Cannon.

On October 11, 1887 Nancy wrote to Mr. Hervey Weeks, a carpenter,

> Do come quick and repair damages for me as soon as the wind gets away from blowing so the north side the house. I must go out and tell you what I want done, my head cannot have wind, it brings on dreadful hard pain, and lasting, bring screws to put on hings, bring one staple. Atrocious damages done me, and besides the damages, the shock of the atrocious damages, has damaged my health, my head feels dreadfully and strength most all gone, and miserable all over, and sick. I wish I never been in this world. I want to go to heaven now. Benjamin Athearn's son tore off top boards off my high yard, and tore off boards above the door, then come over and onfastend the two uper fastens, then him and John Look's son on the other side, tore the door flat on ground, hings off, and split door, and broke all clear, and come in and did many other damages besides destroying my health. Do come as quick as possible, dangerous to have it so. Miss Nancy Luce.

It was Fair time again.

Since practically every household on the Island burned wood, watching smoke was one of the ways

Sketch of Nancy and her homestead by an unknown artist.

that neighbors kept track of one another. Smoke coming from a chimney meant all was well; the family was up and had a fire going. Too much smoke might mean trouble, that the soot in the chimney had caught fire. No smoke could mean that someone was sick and unable to light a fire. But who could see smoke from Nancy's place, or note its absence? She died April 9, 1890. Her obituary in the *Vineyard Gazette* stated she had been "in feeble health for the last two years, yet she lived alone... no one came in from Saturday morning until Monday noon and in the meantime she had fallen and was unable to help herself. After her situation was discovered she was carefully attended to,

67

but soon went into an unconscious state. . . ."

The town advanced the money for her burial. "When I die," she had written Dr. Luce, "somebody will drag me off to Town and burie me there, that must not be." And yet it was; she was buried in West Tisbury Cemetery. She had feared that her age would be misstated. That, too, happened. Her tombstone says she was seventy-nine. She was, in fact, seventy-five. The public had long assumed she was older than she was. "Dont you mind my lieing enemies about my age," she had written Dr. Luce.

Her cow and hens went to William H. Vincent "because he is all the one I have to depend on to attend me in sickness, or any other way, this winter," she had written several years earlier, "he come every day and twice a day, he did not have any pay, he attended to me faithful. . . he is very kind." But he was not to keep the hens. Her will read, ". . .and I request that as soon as I die he chop off the head of every one of my hens. . . . They must suffer no sufferings nor be crueled in any way, nor mourn for me. . . ." Nancy also remembered Mr. Vincent's wife. "To my neighbor Mary Vincent. . . my Yellow Bureau. She has been kind to me when murderers were murdering me. . . ." Could it have been the same bureau with a key to the drawers that Nancy had bought for herself when, a girl, she first went into business? "To George W. Manter of Tisbury, who is the man to see to my graves, all the rest and residue of my Estate both Real and

Personal."

Twelve days after her death, Mr. Manter, whom she named Executor, filed the will at the Dukes County Probate Office. It was never probated, perhaps because she had no real estate, having assigned her property to Dr. Luce years before.

Three years later, February 6, 1893, William J. Rotch, now Selectman of the newly independent town of West Tisbury, replied to a letter from F. H. Day, Esq., of Norwood, Mass.:

> When Miss Nancy died the town was obliged to bury her and owning no real estate the overseers of the poor took her personal effects, but I see no way of realizing the cost unless you will give six dollars for say 30 "Complete Works," 6 or 8 photos like sample, two large do. framed, and a few other pictures. Also an old bible with pen-work and perhaps 50 sheets of composition and pen work. $4. more will take her old bureau which I think is made of mahogany.
>
> Some of the "sheets" are much larger than sample and I judge you can find almost anything you want. Her bible contains a perfect unfaded photo of a different style. $10. for the lot including bureau.
>
> Relatives and others can tell you all about her.

I do not know who the Mr. Day was, why he was interested in Nancy, or if he actually bought the lot. But Nancy's personal effects were sold and these included a small leather trunk filled with all manner of papers.

Half a century later, Ben. C. Clough bought the

trunk and its contents from the Boston bookseller, Charles E. Goodspeed, and gave the whole thing to the Harris collection of American Poetry in the John Hay Library at Brown University. Thus many of her papers wound up in Providence. Many, as I have indicated, remained on the Island, some in West Tisbury with Manter family relatives while other found a snug harbor in Edgartown with the Dukes County Historical Society.

Nancy Luce has her place in the hierarchy of poets.

Photo by Aaron Siskind

Nancy Luce - Her Works

EADING Nancy Luce makes one think of Whitman. She was his almost exact contemporary but they could not possibly have known of one another. Both were born on islands -- on village farms. Both published and sold their own poems, reworked them, and sold them again. Nancy, as noted earlier, also sold photographs of herself and though I do not know that Walt ever did, at one time he planned to. Nancy, like Whitman, wrote in free verse -- not his kind of course, but her own variety -- a rhythmical prose, one might call it, with poetic qualities; in any case something entirely apart from what popular verisifiers and rhymers were turning out. But one cannot compare Nancy Luce to Walt Whitman -- nor to Emily Dickinson, another contemporary with whom she had spiritual and geographical affinites. Whitman and Dickinson stand at one extremity of the literary scale while Luce finds her niche at the other.

A naif, a quasi-folk poet, a phenomenon of the new

71

democratic society where all -- regardless of birth or education -- might take a shot at the arts, Nancy had the right literary impulses. Unable to conform to a schoolbookish English, she wrote in the colloquialisms she spoke, steered clear of conventional subjects, stuck to what she felt and knew: herself, her friends (mostly animals), her enemies (mostly people), and her interpretation of the golden rule, projecting reality as she experienced it.

Written in unsentimental asyntactical language, the emotion in "Poor Little Hearts" speaks straight out. A New England indoor setting, domesticity, maternal love and pride, surrogate children, lost battles with death -- grief and loneliness -- dignity, honesty -- so much rides on what seems to be so little until one takes the symbolism into account. But first the poem itself.

1860.

This heart with a little one in it,
Is to give you to understand,
That hearts can be united.

Hearts aching feeling,
Is a true friend.

Title page of Poor Little Hearts *with author's correction -- the s in penultimate line deleted.*

Poor Little Hearts

Lines composed by Nancy Luce* about poor little Ada Queetie, and poor little Beauty Linna, both deceased. Poor little Ada Queetie died February 25th, Thursday night, at 12 o'clock, 1858, aged most 9 years. Poor little Beauty Linna died January 18th, Tuesday night, most 2 o'clock, 1859, aged over 12 years. She lived 11 months lacking 7 days after poor sissy's decease.

Poor little Ada Queetie has departed this life,
Never to be here no more,
No more to love, no more to speak,
No more to be my friend,
O how I long to see her with me, live and well,
Her heart and mine was united,
Love and feelings deeply rooted for each other,
She and I could never part,
I am left broken hearted.

O my poor deceased little Ada Queetie,
For her to undergo sickness and death,
And the parting of her is more than I can endure,
She knew such a site [sight:lot], and her love and mine,
So deep in our hearts for each other,
Her sickness and death, and parting of her,
I never can get over, in neither body nor mind,
And it may hasten me to my long home,

*The first mention of the author. Her name also appears at the end of the title poem and again on the final page. Only in later editions is her name on the cover.

74

My heart is in misery days and nights,
For my poor deceased little Ada Queetie,
Do consider the night I was left,
What I underwent, no tongue can express.

Poor little Ada Queetie's last sickness and death,
Destroyed my health at an unknown rate,
With my heart breaking and weeping,
I kept fire going night after night, to keep poor little dear warm,
Poor little heart, she was sick one week
With froth in her throat,
Then 10 days and grew worse, with dropsy in her stomach,
I keep getting up nights to see how she was,
And see what I could do for her,
I bathed and birthed* her stomach,
And then give her medicines, but help was all in vain,
Three her last days and nights
She breathed the breath of life here on earth,
She was taken down very sick,
Then I was up all night long,
The second night I was up till I was going to fall,
When I fixed her in her box warm close by the fire,
Put warm clothes under, over, and around,
And left fire burning and lay down with all my clothes on,
A very little while, and got up and up all the time,
The third night I touched no bed at all,
Poor little heart, she was struck with death at
                                     half-past eleven o'clock,
She died in my arms at twelve o'clock at night,
O it was heart-rendering,

*Birthed = berthed: furnished a berth for, held.

75

I could be heard to the road, from that time till daylight,
No tongue could express my misery of mind.

O my heart is consumed in the coffin under ground,
O my heart, my heart, she and I could never part,
Her feelings and mine was so great for each other,
She had more than common love,
And more than common wit,
Her heart was full of love for me,
Now every time I compose a few lines, I have a weeping spell.

O do consider my poor little heart,
She underwent sickness and death,
Deceased and sleeping in her coffin under ground,
O what I undergo for her,
She was my dear, and nearest friend, to love and pity me,
And to believe that I was sick,
She spoke to me, and looked at me most all the time,
And could not go from me.

Poor little heart, she used to jump down to the door to go out.
She would look around, and call me to [go] with her,
She found I could not go, she would come in again,
She loved her dear friendy so well,
She could not go out and leave me.

O my dear beloved little heart,
She was my own heart within me,
When she was well and I was sick, and made out to sit in my chair,
She knew I was sick, because I didn't say but a little to her,
She would stand close to me all the time,
And speak to me, and could not take her eyes of[f] my face,

76

And looked as grieved, as if her heart must break,
She was so worried for me,
And if I was forced to lay down,
Then she was more worried than ever.

When poor little heart happened be out the room,
And I was forced to lay down,
She would come and speak at me, and take on,
As if her heart must break,
And come straight to me, and lament my case,
And would not go from me,
Her feelings was so deeply rooted,
In her heart for me.

Poor little heart, she has been sick 4 times in her lifetime,
I saved her life 3 times, the 4th time, she was taken away,
I was a doctor, and a nurse for her,
And put a little good porridge, and medicines
In her mouth with a tea spoon.

She was coming 9 years of age, when she was taken away,
By all I found out, very certain true,
Poor Sissy hatched her out her egg in Chilmark,
The reason she was taken away before poor Sissy,
Her constitution was as weak as weak could be.

They were brought from Chilmark to New Town,
And remained there one year,
For me to get able to take care of them,
And then they were brought to me.

No one never can replace my poor little hearts, live and well,

No one never can be company for me again,
No one never can I, have such a heart-aching feeling for again,
No one never can I, set so much by again, as I did by them.

Poor little Ada Queetie,
She used to do everything I told her, let it be what it would,
And knew every word I said to her.

If she was as far off as across the room,
And I made signs to her with my fingers,
She knew what it was, and would spring quick and do it.

If she was far off, and I only spake her name,
She would be sure to run to me at a dreadful swift rate,
Without wanting anything to eat.

She would do 34 wonderful cunning things,
Poor Sissy would do 39,
They would do part of them without telling,
And do all the rest of them with telling.

I used to dream distressing dreams,
About what was coming to pass,
And awoke making a dreadful noise,
And poor little Ada Queetie was making a mournful noise,
She was so worried for me,
Then I would speak to her and say, little dear,
Nothing ails your friendy,
Then she would stop and speak a few pretty words to me.

Now I dream about my poor little hearts,
Ever since they were taken away,

78

I dream I see them in my arms, then I dream I cant see them,
And keep asking where is my little dears,
No one speaks for a while, then some one speaks and says,
You never will see them again,
Then I wake taking on at a dreadful rate.

Poor little Ada Queetie,
She used to stand and study out things, she wanted to do,
And then she would go and do it.

She was a patient little heart,
And took everything very kind.

She used to turn first one eye, and then the other to look at me,
When I used to nod my head to her, she would come to me.

She used to get up to the glass, and stand and look sober,
And there fix her feathers, and then look again,
To see if she fixed them right.

When I used to go to the glass to put up my hair,
She would be sure and get up and stand close to my face,
Poor little Beauty Linna did the same, most of the times.

Poor little Ada Queetie,
She always wanted to get in my lap
And squeeze me close up, and talk pretty talk to me.

She always used to want I should hug her up close to my face,
And keep still there she loved me so well.

When she used to be in her little box to lay pretty egg,

It strained me so, I never got over it.

O how I long to see my poor little Beauty Linna live and well,
You know not the company she was for me,
O what a great desire I had for poor little dear to get well,
For she and I to enjoy each others love.

Old age took away poor little Beauty Linna,
Sick over 3 months and grew worse,
With froth in her throat,
Deceased and sleeping in her coffin under ground,
Buried to the south end of poor Sissy's grave,
O how I feel for her,
She was over 12 years of age, when she was taken away,
By all I found out, very certain true.

Poor little heart, never can look at me and laugh,
And speak to me no more
She did it as long as she was able,
She and I talked together, company for each other,
Poor little heart, never can call me back no more,
When I go out the room,
She did it as long as she was able,
For 8 months after poor Sissy's decease,
She would not let me go out the room,
Called me straight back, as soon as I went out,
When 8 months were at a end,
Her complaint began to make her sick.

I fed her with a tea-spoon in her sickness,
Good milk and nutmeg, and good porridge,
Seldom a time in her sickness,
That she could swallow a little good food,

She would be as wishful,
And try to swallow a little good Cake and Cream.

I made fire days and nights to keep poor little dear warm,
The day before poor little dear was taken away,
She opened her eyes and looked up into my face
For the last time,
O my heart is pierced through days and nights,
For my poor deceased little Beauty Linna.

Poor little dear, she could not have the wind to blow on her,
All her last past summer through,
Hurt her so, she would keep out the wind,
She had a sick turn in June by going out a little,
She got over it again.

Poor little dear, she had a very sick turn in August,
I give her medicines, she got over it again,
She shed some of her feathers in September,
And part of them didnt grow out the full length,
She caught cold in October, without being exposed any,
Then her death complaint began to come in.

Some years ago she had one very dangerous complaint,
I cured her very soon, she got well again,
Her complaint that caused her death,
Was just such a complaint as poor Sissy had,
Only poor Sissy's complaint ended with dropsy in her stomach.

A mournful scene it was to me,
To see their breath depart,
Consider soon my turn will come,
And I must follow on,

She would peak up from under the chair,
To see her friendy's face.

When I used to take out account to charge a quart of milk,
She would get up and stand close to me,
And when I told her to shrug up her little shoulders,
She would shrug them up.

She always used to say yesa yesa dear friendy,
I will do just as you say.

She used to do all manner of funny things,
As soon as I told her.

She used to shake my Cape, with all her strength and might,
Every time I told her,
They would both put one foot into my hand,
Every time I told them,
They would both scratch my hand, and pick on my Cape,
Every time I told them.

When some one used to happen to shut them out the room,
They would take on at a dreadful rate,
I let them straight in, and as soon as the person was gone,
Poor little Ada Queetie would not keep out my lap,
Squeezing me up close, talking to me,
Poor little Beauty Linna would not keep off my shoulder,
With her face squeezed close to my face talking to me,
They was so glad they got back in this room with me,
And I wasn't hurt, nor carried away.

Consider those dear little hearts, that loved me so well,
And depended all on me, to be their true friend.

82

When they was both alive, and I had fire in the kitchen
And it come up cold for them,
They would both go in the room, and call me to come to them,
They would stand side and side, and look at the fire-place
                                                  and look at me,
Meaning me to make fire there for them,
Then I would make fire there, and they and I set down together,
Now they are gone, and I am left broken-hearted.

Poor little Beauty Linna has departed this life,
My hands was around her by the fire, my heart aching,
I wept steady from that time till next day,
Poor little heart, she underwent sickness, and death,
Is more than I can endure,
I took the best care of her days and nights,
I did everything that could be done
I did the best that I could do,
I sot up with her nights, till it made me very lame,
When I fixed her in her box warm close by the fire,
Put warm clothes under, over, and around,
And left fire burning and lay down with all my clothes on,
And got up very often with her, and sot up as long as I could,
I never took off none of my clothes for 18 days and nights,
And I did everything to help her complaint,
But help was all in vain,
Medicines could not start her complaint,
Away she must be hurled to pay the debt that we all owe,
Which is to nature due,
They had no sin to answer for, human have that.

I found I could not set up all night at a time, with poor little dear,
As I did the year before, with that poor little dear,
I wept so much the year before,

How can I be here on earth a great while,
I have met with so much trouble of late years.

O I wish my poor little dears could lived longer
And been well, and when they were taken away,
For me to be able to take care of them.

Anxiety of mind will keep any one up and doing,
If they had a friend sick,
If their own health is very miserable,
No one here on earth can know, but only them that knows,
How hard it is to undergo trouble and sickness.

I never can get over the sickness and death,
Of my two poor little Bantie hearts,
They knew such a site, and loved me so well,
And my feelings so great for them both.

My trouble is so hard, that when it begins to be dark,
I set down by the east window, and have a weeping spell,
Then I go to bed, and catch my breath for hours,
I weep by spells day after day,
And night after night for them,
Heart-rendering days and nights.

My poor little hearts have gone to their long home,
And I want to be better off than to be here,
I undergo so much with sickness, and my trouble is so hard.

O my heart is pierced through,
For my poor little hearts to undergo sickness and death,
And for me to part with them, I feel dreadfully.

84

When I am taken away,
I want to be buried to the east side
Of my poor little dear's graves,
And a strong yard made around all three of us together,
And always kept in order, fence and graves too.

When the first poor little heart was taken away,
I had the other poor little heart left,
To sympathize with me, and be company for me,
Now I am left all alone,
After they have lived in the room with me about 8 years,
O how I feel, and how I weep, to write those lines about them,
When poor little Beauty Linna and I was left all alone,
She would set in my lap most all the time,
Her mind was so troubled for poor Sissy
When I sot to the end of the bureau,
She would be sure and get up and set herself down
To the corner of the bureau, with her face close to mine,
There she set would set, as long as I sot there,
When I sot to the fire she would be there.

Poor little heart, she remembered poor Sissy
For 8 months after her decease,
I know it by many things, she sot so much by poor Sissy,
That every time she catched a fly,
She would call with all her strength and might,
For poor Sissy to come and have it,
For Sissy used to do the same by her.

When one got a soft-shell egg broke under her,
She would take hold the tip end of poor Sissy's wing,
And poor poor Sissy knew what she wanted,
And would pick it off for her.

The winter before poor little Beauty Linna was taken away,
Before poor Sissy was taken sick,
She wanted poor Sissy to cover her nights,
She would make a chicken noise,
And run her head in her feathers,
And under poor Sissy's wing.

When I used to go out the room,
And left them both together, and come in again,
They would speak to me, they was so glad I came in again,
And if I was gone too long, they would both call me
To come to them.

When they used to be sitting down, and I looked down on them,
They would tip up their little face on one side,
And look at me with one eye, and laugh and speak to me.

They could not stand any dirt, especially poor little Ada Queetie,
She would snap her mouth and go way broadside

They used to set by the fire close side and side,
Dear little hearts was so tender,
If they meddled with something, I told them you shanty,
They let it alone very willing,
And very seldom they meddled with anything.

If their water happened to be out their little bowl before I knew it,
They would pick on the lower button of the door,
And look at me, for me to get them some water.

Their appetite was always very poor,
Must have the best of good Cake,
And of good wheat, brought from the west.

86

If their cake happened to get out their little plate on the floor,
They could not eat it,
They must have their cake out of my hand or plate.

When they used to see some flies up on the window,
They would stand side and side, and look at me, and call me,
To help them to them flies.

When they used to see me in the new buttery,
They would stand side and side to the door,
And look at me till I came out again.

When I used to call them to turn around,
They would turn around,
When I used to tell them to look at anything,
They would look straight at it.

When I used to say pretty babes,
They would both run to me at a dreadful swift rate,
When I used to say make haste, or come here,
They both did it quick. . . .

Poor little Beauty Linna at last,
Had all the appearance of old age,
She pined away for one year,
And could not stand any cold,
And when she departed this life,
She had all the appearance of old age.

God lent me my beloved friends,
Only to remain with me a few years,
And took them home again.

This world is nothing but a place of trouble,
This world is not our home.

I dream every once in a while,
O how I want my poor little dears
Back again, live and well,
Then I dream I have no desire to have them back,
To undergo sickness and death again.

O my dear beloved little friends, they are gone,
Sweetly asleep in their coffins under ground
No more to wake, no more to speak, no more to love,
No more to have feeling for me,
And I am left here in trouble, broken hearted,
Them that knew me once,
Know -- me -- no -- more.

Ada Queetie and Beauty Linna, like most of her chickens, were bantams, "the bantie sort," Nancy called them. Whatever their breed, perhaps Plymouth Rock, or Rhode Island Red, they were diminutive in size, possibly only twenty-five percent as large as standard fowl. Consequently they were trim, alert, and easy keepers.

In An Illustrated Encyclopedia of Traditional Symbols *(London: Thames and Hudson, 1978) J. C. Cooper writes that a hen symbolizes procreation, providence, maternal care. Further, in Christianity, a hen with chickens depicts Christ with his flock. As I read "Poor Little Hearts," Nancy herself is the symbolic hen while the actual hens are her chicks.*

Eighteen Sixty Six, the Civil War ended, peace restored, Nancy would make another try at having her poems printed. The occasion offered her a chance to invoke a favorite theme again. Also to express (unconsciously, I think) her identification with her animals, the reflectors of her own situation: dependent -- more or less helpless -- bound to the same home place -- an island within an Island.

1866

Be sure and have tender feelings for the poor harmless
                                      dumb creatures,
And not abuse them, and not let them suffer,
And not be cruel them in no way, they can't help themselves,
Consider how you would feel, if you could not help yourselves,
And folks crueld you,
If you had any of the love of God in your hearts,
You would not cruel the poor harmless dumb creatures. . . .

Be sure and do as you wish to be done by,
In deeds, words and thoughts,
To human and to the poor harmless dumb creatures too,
Be sure and not do nor say anything,
To damage, nor plague any one,
Consider, what a wicked thing it is,
Consider, and stamp all wickedness under foot. . . .

Be sure and choose what is right, in the sight of God,
Be sure and not have any evil conduct, and no evil speaking,
Be sure and have no evil thoughts in your hearts,
Be sure and banish it all clear.

Conjured up in a few quick strokes is a swift impression "all in black and white streaks" -- a young Nancy in a transport of speed -- senses, sensations, blurring and mixing.

No Comfort

You don't know how hard it is to me,
Because I cannot ride somewhere,
I cannot ride, nor walk, impossible yet,
I used to ride once in a while,
On a Canter, Gallop and run,
O what comfort that was.

I have had horses to run with me,
So that the ground looked
All in black and white streaks,
There never was a horse
That ever started me from their back,
Now I'm deprived of all comforts of life.

90

Does "the first heart-rendering" death in this characteristic lament refer to the rumored young whaleman?

Sickness

I cannot endure my hard fortune,
To undergo sickness so long,
And cannot ride to have comfort,
I want comfort as well as others.

First cause of destroying my health,
I drove myself with work over 12 years,
Then I met with the first heart-rendering death,
That the work together destroyed my health.

I cannot walk nor stir but a few minutes,
It hurts me so bad,
And I cannot walk on the ground at all,
And I cannot be jared, it hurts me so bad.

If I walk little more one day than common here in the house,
It puts me in great misery for a long while,
And more I stir, more misery I am in,
And most everything hurts me very bad.

I do a few lightest house chores, it hurts me,
I pay out a great deal in hireing work done in the house and out,
I milk my cow, take care of my hens,
I cannot live without cow and hens,
Milk I must have to live on,
Eggs I must have to sell, and a few to use.

A common thing in my sickness,
Milk my cow, take care my hens,
In such misery, I felt as if I must fall at every step,
But I must do it, I must do it.

And a common thing in my sickness,
I was forced to get off the bed sick,
And milk my cow, take care my hens,
Do a little and faint, and going to fall,
And fetch the bed, and get up, and do a little more,
And fail again, get along so,
I could not set up, I was so sick,
I never lay down, without I am going to fall down. . . .

My health has been damaged a few years ago,
A number of times by weeping with death.

And living trouble a number of times,
That racked me at a dreadful rate.

Now you must have pity on me,
And not tell me any distressing news,
It worries me, and weakens me,
And hurts my senses too.

Sickness is a very sad thing to undergo, longer the worse,
Have tender feelings in your hearts,
I am plagued with most every sore disease,
And how can I be cheerful.

Nancy's ingenuity again; an inventive lighthearted use of language that only the animals evoked. With her animals she could be playful. To the world she lamented and complained.

Hen's Names*

Teeddla Toonna.
Phebea Peadeo.
Lebootie Ticktuzy.
Phe endy Tuttaty
Jafy Metreatie.
Shang-go-reany Meleany.
Butturasay Lelowlly.
Oick Cree.
Fasheny Alome.
Fannysay Fainy.
Lily Laly.
Teatalla Meleano.
Tealsa Metdoolsa.
Tweeddleao Tedel.
Levendy Ludandy.
Otte Opheto.
Lilperlaller Laller.
Aterryryree Opacky.

*This list is in her first book, *Poor Little Hearts.* Subsequent editions of *The Complete Works* included others. In all, there are 40 different names.

*Love your neighbor as yourself? Nature and common sense
decree otherwise. I picture Nancy listening politely to what the
neighbors have to say, then making good use of unasked-for
advice in this imagined monologue by an imagined caller. Not
included in* Poor Little Hearts, or A Complete Edition, *it was left
by Nancy along with other manuscripts to a relative, George W.
Manter of West Tisbury. His son, the late Daniel Manter, made it
available to me.*

Unbelievers

Walk out, do you good. You go to neighours.
You do all your work. I glad I found you so comfortable.
I glad I found you so smart. I shall tell I found you well.
I suppose you no courage to do anything.
Put up swing on trees & swing, do you good.
Go south, do you good. Go to campground, do you good.
Take air, do you good. Take my horse & gallop it about.
Take cloth off your head, that is all that ails you.
Eat bread, eat meat, you be well.
Come go out with me or I won't come again. Come ride with me.
You keep your house clean, you do it yourself.
You make lath building yourself. You make butter yourself.
You stick your bean poles yourself.
Take fresh air, do you good.
You go to cattle show. You must come & see me.
You pretty smart. Ride out.
You pretty well. Come down to Edgartown.
You been pretty smart since I saw you last.
I shall tell Dr. when I see him, I found you well.

94

*A poem -- or notes for a poem (among the Manter manuscripts),
Nancy penciled this on a scrap of brown paper, probably in the
1880s. The telegraphic qualities of her verse are striking here --
artful and yet artless. Some awful images in the last three lines
show an ominous dark side of her imagination.*

Red Cannon's Failings

Loud noise. Keep their noise going.
Won't eat blackgrass hay.
Raven for company
Won't come to be milked.
Go dry half their time when with calf.
Kick. Fluk.
Give little milk. Thin milk.
Rank milk. Hold up her milk.
Milk sour quick. Milk hard.
Horns long forward or turn back.
Horns large. Horns sprawl out to sides.
Hook me. Red cow.
 Cream go up top in one night, milk not fit to use.
One part of cow large.*
Skittish.
Jump. Hook down fence.

Mash down fence.
Run head through fence.
Meet cattle to fence and hook it down and won't come away.
Can't be governed when she has unclean spirit in her.
Short teats.
Bloody milk.

*One quarter of the udder.

95

Horse high, hog tight, bull strong -- livestock fenced in, the world fenced out. Nancy's lines, her farm words, verge on poetry.

Fence

A number of folks against my having strong fence, year after year, raven, they say stake it up, it is most impossible to get a man to work on fence, & if I can, it will run everything out, to keep hireing fence tackeld up, next thing down again, when folks get over it. If cow once gets in mischief, then she cant be stopt, in my situation then I done, no milk, I can not live without milk, impossible. I can not live without strong fence so that I can have milk. Milk I must have to live on, or go entirely without eating, & get down sick, & undergo sickness till I die.

This paragraph suggests how the poems may have started -- as an impression and idea in regular prose, later worked out in verse form. Epitomizing Nancy's life and gift, Comparison *could even be her epitaph.*

Comparison

One mouse in torment in the trap, & the rest of the mice runing, taking comfort, this is a comparison to me, to be sick in the house, sick, & other folks riding about, taking comfort, & poor I cant have comfort, consider poor I.

96

*A*ppendix

Four Title Pages

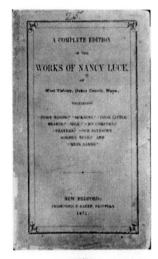

1871

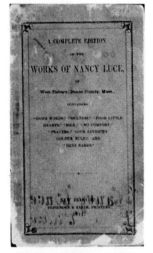

1872

1875

1888

Nancy's Hand-Lettered Work

The fourth page of her booklet headed *Sickness* reads: "Present from Nancy Luce." To whom? Let us say, to readers.

Sickness &c and *Lines Composed by Nancy Luce* that follow seem to have been Nancy's own copies of perhaps the most extraordinary performance in the annals of American diaries. "Be exceeding careful of this Book." While most artists feel that the pain should not show, Nancy evidently felt it should.

Nancy made the cover for the 4 1/4 by 2 1/2 inch booklet from a bit of wallpaper (opposite). She had already used the back side of it for a draft of "Poor Little Hearts" which shows .

5 or 6 years ago, by having help of Dr Luce. A. am easy hurt. A. feel miserably. A. do a few lightest house chores, that hurts me. A. have complaints all over me.

Many & many has been the time I milked my Cow & took care my hens, & felt as if I must fall at every step, I was so sick, but I must do it. I must do it.

A. cannot live without Cow & Hens, impossible.

They wont allow me to raise Clover to have profit of the Cow fall & winter. They damage me. My hay wont make much milk.

I could sell a great deal of butter, & milk too, fall & winter. Summer I cant sell either.

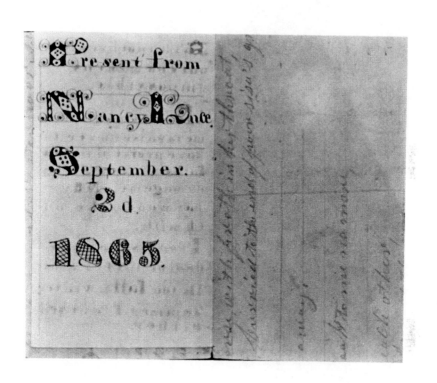

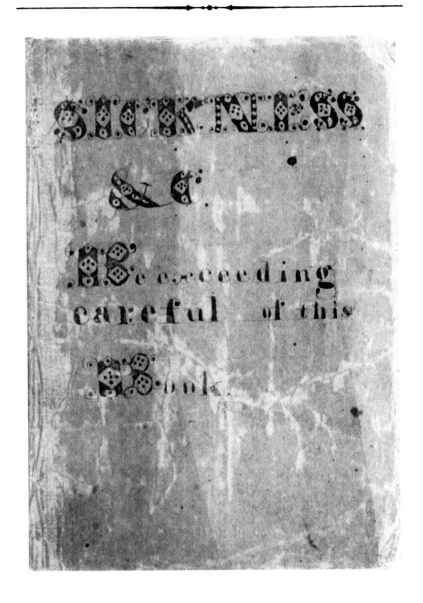

SICKNESS
&c

Be exceeding careful of this Book.

102

SICKNESS.

I can't bear up sickness to undergo, year after year, distressing, and can't ride somewhere to have comfort, consider poor I. I can't stand, walk, but a few minutes here in the house, it hurts me dreadfully on the account of lameness. My health has been destroyed a number of times by weeping with death a few years ago. Weeping strains me. I wept the most in 1858, with heart rending death, destroyed my health. Now 1865, my health is good deal better than it was 5 or 6 years ago, by having help of

Dr Hyce. I am easy hurt. I feel miserably. I have complaints all over me. I cant arn anything. I do a few lightest house chores it hurts me. Any exercising or jaring, hurts me. I cant sturb but a little, on the account of lameness, & other complaints too. more I stur, more misery I am in, stiller I keep, better it is for me. I cant walk on the ground that is worse than the floor. I cant lay out but a very little strength to do anything, it hurts me. I cant do anything the least jurking, it hurts me. I cant have any one to walk heavy by my Chair, it jars me, hurts my lameness. I cant lift but a little, it hurts me. Consider poor I.

can't bear up sickness.

A few years ago, it put me in dreadful misery, to bend forward, or bend back, or twist myself a little around, &c. now I am better. but it hurts me some yet. Some times it hurts me great deal more, than it does another time.

First cause of destroying my health, I drove myself with work over 12 years, then I met with the first heart-rending death, in 1840, that & the work together, destroyed my health, then I underwent a dreadful site with sickness 10 years, Dr Bruce helpt my health a number of times, & I was getting better as fast as could be expected then meet with either death, or living trouble, mostly death to make me weep, that would destroy my health again, & grow worse, till I got help of Dr Huce again. Distressing to undergo misery of mind, & misery of body, & no comfort in this world. Consider poor H. Since I lost my health, I have met with living trouble a number of times, it racked me most out this troublesome world.

When 1850, Dr Huce cured some very dangerous complaints for me, that I underwent a dreadful site with, & helpt the rest of them some, so that I get along as I have since, that is, my health gets damaged every once in a while & forced to get help of Dr Huce again. H. cant bear up sickness

106

I undergo a great deal more with sickness some days & nights than I do others, I don't know the reason of that.

Every time I have seen a horse going on a canter, since I lost my health, I have a weeping spell, because it is so hard to me, because I can't ride so.

Distressing news worries me, & hurts my senses too.

I am forced to pay out over $50 a year in hireing work done in the house & out, & all my expenses, except the expense I am to the Doctor, I dont reckon that.

When I first fenced in my land, & shingled my house, then I payed out most a hundred dollars a year, for over two years.

I have had great pull backs, besides twenty five years sickness, a number of pull-backs, one thing is, as soon as my poor father was gone, they layed heavyer taxes on me, beach taxes, Chilmark taxes, home place taxes, and kept it private from me, till they had heapt up a large amount, then threatend to take some my land. See how they served me. Some have fought in every way, to stop my keeping a cow, that I cannot live without.

I milk my cow, & take care my hens, that I must do, as long as I can put one foot before the other

& when I cannot put one foot before the other, no longer, then I shall die.

I cannot live without Cow & Hens, impossibe.

Many & many has been the time I milk'd my Cow, & took care my hens, & felt as if I must fall at every step, I was so sick, but I must do it, I must do it.

And many & many has been the time, I been forced to get off the bed sick, & milk my Cow, & take care my hens, & do a little, & going to fall, I was so sick, & so faint, & fetch the bed before I fell on the floor, & then get up, & do little more & fail again, that was the way I

I was forced to do, in my sickness
part my time, forced to. Consider
poor I.

I can't bear up sickness, to undergo
year after year, & no enjoyments,
Consider poor I.

COMPARISON

One mouse in torment in the trap,
& the rest of the mice runing taking
comfort, this is a comparison to me, to
be in the house sick, & other folks riding about, taking comfort, & poor I
can't have comfort, Consider poor I.

WOODLEY

THINK IS

A DOCTOR.

When I tell folks about being sick, some of them say, you must have some wood, there see, as if wood skillful Doctor to cure dangerous complaints. and some say did you get some cold, &c&c. See how much they believe.

TROUBLE.

A few years back, a few relation, a few besides, every time they found me in heart-rending trouble, they threatend me, abused me, so hard as trouble is, they made me weep dreadfully, destroyed my health. Those folks never come to sympathize with me in trouble, and never come to see what they could do for me in sickness, but they all come raven, & told me all distressing news, it worried me, &hurt my health &hurt my senses. They was cruel to me.

Some folks no feeling for me, unbelieving against me in sickness.

STOVE.

They abuse me to spend every thing in stove & wood to set by, I wont, I need other things hundred times more. Wood won't warm me in winter nor strengthen me, milk porridge will warm me, &strengthen me too. Milk is cooli g to health, & strengthening.

FENCE.

A number of folks against my having strong fence, year after year, raven, they say stake it up, it is most impossible to get a man to work on fence, & if I can, it will run every thing out, to keep hireing fence tackeld up, next thing down again, when folks get over it, If Cow once gets in mischief, then she cant be stopt, in my situation then I done, no milk, I can not live without milk, impossible. I cannot live without strong fence, so that I can have milk.

Milk I must have to live on, or go entirely without eating, & get down sick, & undergo sickness till I die.

How would you feel to be served
so bad as I am, Every thing I under
take to have done, to be a great help
to me to get along, some folks rave
against it, & stop it, I can't lives
I could get along first rate, if I wa
s allowed to. They don't like I sho
ld have anything but wood to se
by, I am tried.

That I don't want, & don't need,
they raven for me to get.
That I want, & need, they rav-
en against. I am tried.

READ THIS.

If I was allowed to raise
Clover hay, & clover fall fee
I could have every thing I need

because I can sell a great deal of butter, & milk too, fall & winter. Summer, I can't sell either I could get along first rate. and the clover would save my paying a great deal in buying spoilt dead fodder, at full price, & hireing the black grass salt hay saved, this 18 years, that wont make cow give much milk.

Some folks have damaged me great_ly, in stoping my making clover mead_ow.

Now I have a little clover, they would not save it for me, for money down, nor on a lay, till the juice was most all out, stop my having milk for profit, then they saved it for pay.

They wont allow me to have anything with the juice in it, to give the cow fall & winter, to have profit of the cow, they won't allow it, They damage me.

Their law is raven, for cow to have all the land in summer, stop my getting cow to milk, & stop my raising clover for winter, to have profit of the cow, & save expense. I am tried.

They eat swine's flesh, that is the reason they dont like I should raise clover.

HENS.

Some folks against my keeping hens, & against my feeding them, & against my keeping them warm, they dont care how much poor hens suffer with hunger, & cold, stop my having eggs to help myself with. I cannot live without hens.

They cruel to their poor hens.

HOW WOULD YOU FEEL TO BE SERVED SO BAD AS I AM.

Some folks against my having
help of the Doctor, to get better.
against my having strong fence
to have milk. against my raising
Clover, to have milk fall & winter
for profit, & save expense.
against my having my new barn
Clean. Against my having a seller, for poor hens to be comfortable, & for me to have eggs to help m-
yself with, & save my hurting
myself taking care my hens, &
have apartment to keep things
from frost. Against my having
pine trees around the house, to
keep wind off the house. Three
against my Book being printed
against my keep a Cow.
against my having things

in the house like other folks, &c&c.
How would you feel, to be served so, by
some folks.

CLOVER & KNOWN-

OTTINGS & AGA-

INST ME.

They raven against my raising
Clover, because three growths to clover,
mow it twice in the summer, as soon as
it comes into bloom, that is the time to
mow it to get milk, and second grawth
is the sweetest to make milk, &
best time to take it in cooler, I don-
t want much hay in, when hot weather,

be another growth for fall feed for profit. For these reasons, they don't like I should raise Clover. a few of them like I should raise herds grass, there see, because that only comes in first the summer. I am tried. I want to raise Clover hay, & Clover fall feed, Clover hay to give the Cow after the grass is gone, to have profit of the Cow, & save expense. And save some Clover hay, to give the Cow in May & first of June. I want to raise red top to mix with the salt hay to give the Cow later part of the winter. Plan for profit. You all know that after the summer grass is gone, wont any cow eat salt hay, she will dry off with hunger, & if she did eat it, it wont make much milk. Then it is time of profit with milk.

I could get along first rate, if I was allowed to.

COW, & HARDNESS, & DOWN FALL.

When my old Cow come to nothing by old age, & didnt give milk enough for me to live on, & no milk & butter to sell, then all that year & half expenses heapt up, great pull back to me. I asked all the folks I saw, and Dr Luce asked all over the Island, they would not let me have a cow. Dr Luce, & I asked all that time. A number of men had new milch heifers, & farrow heifers they wanted to change away to get a cow to fat, & would not change with me, because they wanted to get me down sick for want of milk, & stop my getting along too. at last Dr Luce made out to get a farrow heifer, & she could nt be new milch, then Dr Luce asked again all over the Island, & they would not let me have a Cow, See how against me. Then Dr Luce sent me one of his good Cows, & took the heifer, no one else would done so well by me. Dr Luce has saved my life a number of times, in differant ways, & helpt me to have something to help myself with. That cow he let me have was the best Cow for milk & butter, I ever had. Then human caused something to happen to her. Now I have another Cow, Mr Josiah H Vincent made out to get for me, had hard work to get a heifer for me.

Some folks so against me, they against my keeping a cow, and against my having anything I need dreadfully. They wicked folks.

LAW.

The law is raven against my getting good deal to have on hand, for hens to eat, & myself, & against my getting anything till I am out. I cannot go impossible, & most impossible to send, some times. Consider I must have enough on hand for poor hens to eat, & not be catched, Consider. I must have eggs to help myself with.

KNOW NOTHINGS
TURN WANTS.

Within 13 years, 7 folks have asked me raven to let them come here & live, they impose on me. They would destroy everything. and drive my hens in woods, I cannot live without hens. and the whole house

& every thing in it, would be nasted & stink with hog-swine's grease, I could not live in the house. I must have every thing clean. I never will take in no one.

SICKNESS DOWN FALLS.

My poor father used to own property enough, he arn't it himself, he owned english meadow in Tisbury & in West Tisbury, His sickness & my poor mother's sickness, a number of years, caused him to sell all his english meadow, part his wood land, part his clear land, a great flock of sheep, young cattle, a pair of great oxen, a horse, some cows, &c&c. to get money to pay a number of Doctors, & folks to stay with mother a number of years, most of this was when I was a little girl. Their last sickness cost a great deal, a great deal wood land & clear land sold then. See what sickness is. Father used to be a worker when he was able, & very saving, but when he had dealings with folks, he always used to give them the best of the bargain, to help them along, & besides that, he used to give folks. I think he was a Christian later part of his days, gone to heaven.

UNBELIEF.

When I die, you must not say that I died sudden, my complaints enough to ware me out, I never

lay down day time, without I am
going to fall down, I always put
myself forward all that lays in
my power, I never give back,
without I am forced to.

Them that calls on me, must come with good hearts, tender feelings, speak the trut-
h, to my face, & behind my
back, but gross sinners
must keep away.
Strive for the love of God in
your hearts.

Nancy Louce.

1865.

Lines composed by Nancy Luce about poor little Ada Queta, and poor little Beauty Linna, both deceased, poor little Ada Queta died the 25th of FEBRUARY thursday night 1858, poor little Beauty Linna died the 18th of JANUARY, tuesday night 1859. She lived 11 months lacking 7 days after poor sisa's decease.

Poor little Ada Queta has departed this life
Never to be here no more,
Never to love, nor speak to me, nor be my friend no more
O how i long to see poor sisa with me live and well
Her heart and mine was united,
Love and feelings deeply rooted for each other
She and i could never part
I am left broken hearted.

O do consider my poor little heart,
She underwent sickness and death
Deceased and sleeping in her coffen under ground
O what i undergo for her,
She was my dear and nearest friend, to love and pity
And to believe that i was sick
She spake to me, and looked at me most all the time
And could not go from me.

Poor little Ada Queta,
She used to jump down to the door to go out
She would look around, and call me to go with her
She found i could not go, she would come in again
She loved her dear friend so well, she could not go out and
leave me.

O my dear beloved little heart, she was my own heart [within me
When she was well, and i was sick,
And made out to set in my Chair,
She knew i was sick because i did nt say but a very little to [her,
She would stand close to me all the time,
and speak to me and would not take her eyes of my face,
And look as grieved as if her heart must break,
She was so worried for me,
And if i was forced to lay down,
Then she was more worried than ever.

When poor little Ada happend to be out the room,
and i was forced to lay down,
She would come and peak at me, and take on,
As if her heart must break,
and come straight to me, and lament my case
would not go from me,
her feelings was so deeply rooted,
in her heart for me.

heart she has been sick 4 times, in her life time,
saved her life 3 times, the 4th time she was taken away,
was a doctor and a nurse for her,
and put good porridge in her mouth with a ten- [spoon,
She was coming 9 years old, when she was taken aie-[ay,
By all i found out very certain true,
instead of coming 8, as i only called her.
The reason she was taken away first
her constitution was as weak as weak could be
poor sisa hatched her out of her egg in Chilmar-[k.

They was brought from Chilmark to New Town
And remained there one year
For me to get able to take care of them,
And then they were brought to me.

No one never can replace my poor litdle dears live and well
No one never can be company for me again,
No one never can i have such a heart aching feeling for
No one never can i set so much by again, as i did by them, again,

The parting of my poor little Ada Queta
I never can get over, in neither body nor mind
And it may hasten me to my long home,
And for her to undergo sickness and death
Is more than i can endure,
She knew such a site, and her love and mine
So deep in our hearts, for each other
My heart is in misery days and nights
For my poor deceased little Ada Queta
To consider the night i was left,
What i underwent, no tongue can express.

Her last sickness and death destroyed my health
At a unknown rate, with my heart breaking
I kept fire going night after night, [and weeping
To keep poor little dear warm

Poor little heart
She was sick one week with froth in her throat,
Then ten days and grew worse,
With dropsy in her stomach,
I kept getting up nights to see how she was,
And see what i could do for her,
3 the last days and nights, she was taken down very
Then i was up all night long,   [sick,
She second night i was up, till i was going to fall,
Then i fixed her in her box, warm close by the fire,
Put warm Clothes under, over, and around
And left fire burning, and lay down,
With all my Clothes on, a very little while,
And got up, and up all the time,
The third night i touched no bed at all,
Poor little heart, she was struck with death at half pas,
She died in my arms, twelve o clock at night,   eleven
O it was heart rending,
I could been heard to the road from that time till day
No tongue could express, my misery of mind.   light

O my heart is consumed in the Coffen under ground
She and i could never part till death took her away
Now every time i compose a few lines, i have a weep
She had more than Common love, and more than com
Her heart was full of love for me,   mon wit

She used to do everything i told her let it be what it would
And i knew every word i said to her,
If she was as far off as across the room
And i made signs to her with my fingers
She knew what it was, and would spring quick and
                                              do it,
If she was ever so far off and i only spake her name
She would be sure and run tome at a dreadful swift rate
Without wanting anything to eat eat .

I used to dream distressing dreams
About what was coming to pass,
And awoke making a dreadful noise,
And poor little Ada Queta was making a mournful
She was so worried for me,   noise
And then i would speak to her and say, little dear,
Nothing ails your frienda,
Then she would stop and speak a few pretty words to
                                              me,

Now i dream about my poor little hearts,
Ever since they were taken away,
I dream i see them in my arms,
Then i dream i cannot see them,
And keep asking where is my little dears
No one speaks for a while, then some one will speak and
You never will see them again,   say,
Then i awake taking on at a dreadful rate .

Poor little Beautey Hanna has departed this life
Most 2 o clock at night my hands around her by the fire
I wept steady from that time till next day my heart aching
She underwent sickness and death,
Is more than i can endure,
I took the best of care of her days and nights,
I did everything that could be done,
I did the best that i could do,
I sot up nights with her till it made me very lam,
When i fixed her in her box warm close by the fire
Put warm clothes under over and around
And left fire burning and lay down
With all my clothes on,
And got up very often with her
And sot up as long as i could
I never took off none of my clothes for 18 days and nights
And i did everything to help her complaint
But help was all in vain,
Medicines could not start her complaint,
Away she must be hurled to pay the debt that we all owe
Which is to nature due.

O how i long to see her with me live and well
My heart aches within me
You know not the company she was for me,
O what a great desire i had for her to get well
For she and i to enjoy each others love.

God lent me my beloved friends,
Only to remain with me a few years
And took them home again
O my dear beloved friends they are gone
And i am left all alone here in trouble
Them that knew me once, know me no more.

Old age took away poor little Beauty Lina
Sick over 3 months and grew worse
With froth in her throat
Deceased and sleeping in her coffen under ground
Buried to the end of poor sisa's grave 0 how i feel for her
She was over 12 years old when she was taken away
By all i found out very certain true,
Instead of coming 9 as i only called her,

Poor little dear never can look at me and laugh
And speak to me no more she did it as long as she was able
She and i talked together company for each other
Poor little dear never can call me back no more
When i go out the room she did it as long as she was able
For 8 months after poor sisa's decease
She would not let me go out the room
Called me straight back, as soon as i went out
When 8 months were at a end her complaint began to make her sick,
i fed her with a teaspoon in her sickness,
Good milk and nutmeg, and good porridge
Seldom a time in her sickness,
That she could swallow a little good food
She would be as wishful and try to swallow
A little good cake and cream.

I made fire days and nights to keep poor little dear [warm]
The day before poor little dear was taken away
She open'd her eyes, and looked me up into my face for [the last time]
My heart is pierced through days and nights
For my poor deceased little Beautyfulina.
I never can get over the sickness and death
Of my two poor little Bantie hearts,
They knew such a site, and loved me so well
And my feelings so great for them both
My trouble is so hard that whan i go to bed
I catch my breath for hours
Heart rending days and nights.
My poor little hearts have gone to their long [home]
And i want to go too,
I feel dreadfuly for them to undergo sickness [and death]
And for me to part with them
I feel dreadfuly dreadfuly, it seems as if i [must die.]
When i am taken away
I want to be buried to the south end
Of my poor little dear's graves
And a strong yard made around
All 3 of us together.
When the first poor little heart was taken away,
I had the other poor little heart left,
To sympathize with me, and be company for me
Now i am left all alone alonea,
After they have lived in the room with me
About 8 years.

134

When poor little Beauty Lina and i was left all
alone
She would set in my lap most all the time
Her mind was so troubled for poor sisa
When i sot to the end of the bureau
She would be sure and get up and set her self down
In the corner of the bureau
With her face close to mine
There she would set as long as i sot there
When i sot to the fire she would be there.

She could not have the wind to blow on her
All this last past summer through,
It hurt her so, she would keep out the wind
She had a sick turn in June by going out a
little
She got over it again.

She had a very sick turn in August
I give her medicines she got over it again
She shed some of her feathers in september
And part of them did nt grow out the full
length
She took Cold
October her death complaint begun to come
on.

Some years ago she had one very dangerous
complaint
I cured her very soon she got well again
Her complaint that caused her death
Was just such a complaint as poor sisa had
Only poor sisa's complaint
Ended with dropsy in her stomach.

135

Anxiety of mind will keep any one up and doing
If they have a friend sick if their own health is very
No one here on earth can know, but only them that knows miserable
How hard it is to undergo trouble and sickness.

Poor little Beauty Lina remembered poor sis
For 8 months after her decease   a
I know it by many things,
She set so much by poor sisa,
That every time she catched a fly,
She would call with all her strength and mig-
For poor sisa to come and have it   ht
Poor sisa used to do the same by her.

The winter before poor little Beauty Lina was tak
Before poor sisa was taken sick   en away
She wanted poor sisa should hover her nights,
She would make a chicken noise,
And run her head in her feathers,
And under poor sisa's wing.

Poor little Ada Queta always used to say
Yesa yesa dear frienda,
I will do just as you say,
She used to do all manner of cunning things
As soon as i told her.

She used to shake my cape with all her strength an
Every time i told her   might
They would both put one foot into my hand
Every time i told them
They would both scratch my hand
And peck on my cape,
Every time i told them.

136

When i used to go out the room,
And left them both together
And come in again they would speak to me,
They was so glad i come in again,
If i was gone tolong,
They would both call me to come to them.

When they used to be setting down,
And i looked down on them
They would tip up their little face on one side
And look at me with one eye
And laugh and speak to me.

Poor little Ada Queta she used to get up to the glass
And stand and look sober
And then fix her feathers,
And then look again
To see if she fixed them right.

When i used to go to the glass to put up my hair
Poor little Ada Queta would be sure and get up
And stand close to my face,
Poor little Beauty Hina did the same
Most of the times.

Poor little Ada Queta,
She used to stand and study out things she
She wanted to do, and then she would go and do it.
She was a patient little heart
And took everything very kind.

She used to turn first one eye,
And then the other to look at me.
When i used to nod my head to her,
She would come to me.

She always used to want to get in my lap,
And squeeze me close up
And talk pretty talk to me.

She always used to want i should hug her up
Close to my face and keep still there
She loved me so well.

When she used to be in her little box to lay pretty
She would peak up from under the cha. egg
To see her friends face. ir

When i took out account to charge a quart of in.
She would get up and stand close to me
When i told her to shrug up her little shoulders
She would shrug them up.

They could not stand any dirt
Especially poor little Ada Queta,
She would snap her mouth
And go way broad side.

They used to set by the fire,
Close side and side
Dear little hearts was so tender.

If they meddled with something,
I told them you shan'ta,
They let it alone very willing
And seldom they meddled with anything.

138

If their water happened to be out their little bowl
Before i knew it
They would peck on the lower button
And look at me, for me to get them some water.

Their appetites was always very poor,
Must have the best of good cake
And best of new wheat brougt from the west.

If their cake happened to get out their little plate on the floor
They could not eat it
They must have their cake out of my hand or plate.

They used to see some flys upon the window
They would stand side and side and look at me
And call me to help them to their flys.

When they used to see me in the new buttery
They would stand side and side to the door
And look at me till i come out again.

When i used to tell them to turn around,
They would turn around
When i told them to look at anything
They would look straigt at it.

When i used to say pretty babes,
They would both run to me,
At a dreadful swift rate.
When i used to say make haste
Or come here,
They both did it quick.

When one got a soft shell egg broke under
She would take hold the tip end   her
Of poor sisa's ?ing
And poor sisa knew what she wanted
And would pick it off for her.

When they was both alive and i had fire in the
And it come up to cold for them   kitchen
They would go in the rooms
And call me to come to them
They would stand side and side
And look at me and look at the fire place
Beaming me to make fire there for them
When i would make fire there
And they and i set down together.

O how i wish they could lived longer
And been well
And when they was taken away
For me to be able to take care of them

When some one used to happen
To shut them out the room,
They would take on at)(a drea
I let them straight in)   [rate,
And as soon as the person was gone
Poor little Zilda Queta
Would not keep out my lap,
Squeezeing me close up, talking to me,
Poor little Beauty Lima.
Would not keep of my shoulder
With her face squeezed close against my
Talking to me,   [face,
They was so glad they got back in the
Into the room with me,
And wasn't hurt nor carried away,
Consider these dear little hearts
That loved me so well,
And depended all on me to be their
                              [true friend,

141

When i first had them a man told me it was his opinion that poor little Beauty Lina was old what he knew and another man told me he knew ... bit she was quite old when she was brought from Chilmark to New town and she hatched poor little Ada Queta out of her egg in Chilmark and she was over a year old when she was brought from Chilmark and coming 9 years old when she was taken away and poor little Beauty Lina was over 12 years old when she was taken away

I did this Book in misery in both body and mind, in July and August 1859.

Nancy Luce

BIBLIOGRAPHY

Anonymous, *A Guide to Martha's Vineyard and Nantucket.* Boston: Rockwell & Churchill, Printers, 1878.

Anonymous, The Contributors' Club, "Hens and their Laureate," *Atlantic Monthly,* July 1892, pp. 142-44.

Anonymous, The Contributors' Club, "A Visit to the Laureate of Hens," *Atlantic Monthly,* October 1892, pp. 572-73.

Block, William J., "The Nancy Luce Guardianship Papers," *Dukes County Intelligencer,* Edgartown, Massachusetts, February 1978.

Clough, Ben C., "Poor Nancy Luce," *The New Colophon,* September 1949.

Goodspeed, Charles E., *Yankee Bookseller.* Boston: Houghton Mifflin Company, 1937, pp. 95, 97.

Hine, C. G., *The Story of Martha's Vineyard.* New York: Hine Brothers, 1908, pp. 179-80.

Hough, Dorris S., "Some Vineyard Authors," *Dukes County Intelligencer,* May 1962.

Hough, George A., "Nancy Luce," unsigned undated pamphlet reprinted from New Bedford *Standard,* May 19, 1907.

Hough, Henry Beetle, *Martha's Vineyard Summer Resort 1835-1935.* Rutland, Vermont: The Tuttle Publishing Company, Inc., 1936, pp. 139-44.

Huntington, Gale, "Nancy Luce," *Dukes County Intelligencer,* May 1969.

Luce, Nancy, *Poor Little Hearts,* facsimile reprint by the Dukes County Historical Society, 1969.

Teller, Walter, "The Time and the Place," *The American Scholar,* XXXV. 3, Summer 1966.

Teller, Walter, *Cape Cod and the Offshore Islands.* Englewood Cliffs: Prentice-Hall, Inc., 1970, pp. 112-24.

Teller, Walter, *Twelve Works of Naive Genius.* New York: Harcourt Brace Jovanovich, Inc., 1972, pp. 152-66.

ACKNOWLEDGEMENTS

Warm thanks to Nahoma Clinton, Florence Crowther, and Arthur R. Railton for counsel and helpful suggestions; to John Hersey, William Howarth, Edward Huberman, Peggy Lewis, Alicia Ostriker, and Jane Teller for reading the manuscript and advising; to Aaron Siskind for photographs; to Margaret Barnes and Virginia Gosselin for decorative lettering; and to Norma E. H. Bridwell for her drawing.

I am indebted to Betty Vas Nunes Burroughs for long-time assistance and moral support.

W. M. T.

CPSIA information can be obtained at www.ICGtesting.com
Printed in the USA
BVOW05s0555260814

364264BV00005B/209/P